ABOUT the AUTHOR

John Purner is an avid pilot, golfer, publisher, website developer and writer. His **$100 Hamburger** website *(www.100dollarhamburger.com)* has been the most popular website for recreational flyers for more than two decades. John's first work of fiction, **02 Golf** has been an aviation category Best Seller since its publication two years ago.

The following is a list of other John Purner books you may enjoy. They are available at Amazon.com and pilot shops across the world.

1. **02 GOLF**

2. **6 Weeks to Winning Weekend Golf**

3. **BUYcycle: The Best Kept Secrets of Amazingly Successful Salespeople**

4. **15 BEST Airport Restaurants plus 2,347 Runner-Ups!**

5. **The $100 Hamburger – A Guide to Pilots' favorite FlyIn Restaurants 3rd Edition**

6. **101 Best Aviation Attractions**

7. **The $100 Hamburger – A Guide to Pilots' favorite FlyIn Restaurants 2nd Edition**

8. **The $500 Round of Golf : A Guide to Pilot-Friendly Golf Courses**

9. **The $100 Hamburger – A Guide to Pilots' favorite FlyIn Restaurants**

The $100 Hamburger

Guide to
Buying and Selling Aircraft

By
John Purner

$100 Hamburger Publishing

ISBN-13: 978-0615926995 ($100 Hamburger Publishing)
ISBN-10: 0615926991

For quantity discounts on volume orders please contact

$100 Hamburger Publishing
PO Box 915441
Longwood, FL 32791-5441

Internet: www.100dollarhamburger.com
Email: pirep@100dollarhamburger.com

First Printing: November 2013

Preface

Two things make this is the best time in the history of earth to buy a used general aviation aircraft.

First, the asking prices for used airplanes offered for sale are at an all-time low when adjusted for inflation and seen as a percentage of the purchase price of a similar new aircraft.

Second, money is cheaper than it has ever been. The Federal Reserve is currently making money available to its member banks at zero (0) percent interest. It is not possible to get a lower interest rate than zero unless they start paying the banks to haul away their cash. There is one caveat. By the time that money reaches you or anyone else that wants to borrow it the banks have added an amazing markup. I recently borrowed a wad of cash for slightly under three percent. That's the lowest rate I or anyone living has ever paid. It is still an amazingly sweet deal for the banks. I'm fine with that and you should be too.

Low airplane prices and cheap money make a perfect storm for airplane buyers. Get onboard soon though, as this train is leaving the station. If you take nothing else away from this book, I hope you will latch on to that. Today is your day not someday.

Finding the airplane you want is a problem. You can't order a used airplane from the used airplane factory in the color you want equipped exactly as you desire at the price you are willing to pay. This book is written to help make the hunt easier and more productive.

Making a good buy is tough but doing so will make the job of selling easy. If you're like me you'll probably have to sell something to buy something else. Most hangars and wallets can accommodate only one airplane at a time. The last section of the book deals with selling.

My primary focus is on traditional certified, experimental and LSA piston engine singles and light twins. Jets and turbo props are bought and sold the same way with one major caveat. Few are sold directly by the owner. Typically, jets and turbo props are offered by agents, brokers or dealers. That is a significant point.

The issues associated with purchasing a jet or a turbo prop are one order of magnitude more involved as they have complex systems that are not associated with piston aircraft. For instance, their engines have maintenance schedules that will be foreign to most mere mortals.

A jet's life is not so much measured by total time but importantly by the number of landing and takeoff operations it has executed. When a maintenance issue surfaces with a jet or turbo prop the cost of addressing it can be humongous.

Buying a jet or turbo prop without engaging a respected consultant is a big mistake. Finding the right consultant is made easier by joining the type club that supports the aircraft you're interested in. For example, join the **Citation Jet Pilots** if you fancy a Citation. Their members will be glad to send you the name, contact information and rating of the consultants that work with Citation buyers.

If jets are the high end, LSAs are the theoretical low end. This book includes LSAs and Experimentals in our buying and selling approach as you can expect to work directly with the owner or purchaser.

The **L**ight **S**port **A**ircraft world is made up of two groups. The first is those that have been recently manufactured by one of the 100 or so worldwide companies that answered the call when the FAA announced the LSA program. The others are fairly ancient certified flying machines that happen to meet the LSA specification and can be legally flown as either a certified aircraft or as an LSA. My personal favorite is the Ercoupe 415C.

The oddity of the LSA world is the Piper J3 Cub. The real ones are included with the ancient flyers; several newly manufactured copies crowd the other group, most allow the pilot to sit in the front seat unlike the original.

Many pilots who have lost their medical or are about to lose their medical wrongly believe that buying and flying an LSA as a Sport Pilot is a way to keep them in the air.

It isn't.

A great benefit of the LSA program is the ability for pilots who have a current driver's license to self-certify their medical condition. It allows us to fly without a medical **IF** we believe that we are medically fit and have no medical conditions that would prevent us from flying or exclude us from passing an FAA medical examination. It doesn't allow us to fly LSA if we **KNOW** that we can't pass the FAA Medical. If you have a heart condition that prevents you from getting a 3rd Class Medical, you can't certify that you are medically fit to fly an LSA even if you have a current driver's license.

Read this writing from the **FFA - Federal Air Surgeon**

"Long-standing FAA regulation, 61.53, prohibits all pilots--those who are required to hold airman medical certificates and those who are not--from exercising privileges during periods of medical deficiency. The FAA revised 61.53 to include under this prohibition sport pilots who use a current and valid U.S. driver's license as medical qualification. The prohibition is also added under 61.23 (c) (2) (iv) and 61.303 (b) (2) (4) for sport pilot operations."

The center section of this book includes some photos I call **My Favorites**. These are some of the planes that I have owned and flown over the years. A few of the photos are of actual airplanes that I have loved others are of sister ships as I sadly lost most of my treasured airplane photos due to a computer hard drive crash. I learned a lesson about backing up files.

You will notice that many wonderful airplane types are missing; the Beech Bonanza is an example. Frankly, I have never owned one. I always wanted too and maybe someday I will.

A few airplanes that I have owned are also missing from the center section. The Cessna 150 is an example. I simply didn't have access to a photo that I could legally use. That's sad as I even based a novel titled **02 Golf**, about my adventures in the one I owned. The Kindle version of the book is still an **AVIATION BEST SELLER** on Amazon.com.

Occasionally we airplane buyers are presented with a dilemma. Do we spend as much for a perfect Cessna 172 as we could buy a flawed Cessna 182 for? The answer to that question is within each owner/pilot's mind. The goal of this book is to help you get what you want not to tell you what you should want.

The purchase of this book includes a **FREE** one year subscription *($17.95 value)* to my **$100 Hamburger** website **www.100dollarhamburger.com**. It has been around for two decades and is the favorite website of recreational flyers.

To get your logon credentials simply send an email to me at jpurner@100dollarhamburger.com. You must attach some form of proof of purchase. Anything that lets me know that you purchased the book will do.

Fly someplace today. You've earned it!

Table of Contents

BUY LOW

SELL HIGH

BUY LOW

Chapter I

It's Expensive to be Cheap

The Big Idea: Finding the ship you want and paying the bucks to get it is the **ONLY** way to go.

There is no bigger fool than the girl who marries a guy believing she can "fix" his flaws and turn him into the "perfect" husband. Buying an airplane with a few "fixable issues" is a trip down that same rabbit hole.

Rule number one in aircraft buying is to always **buy with an eye towards selling**. If you can't buy it today and sell it tomorrow at a profit, don't buy it! That's easier said than done, of course. Here's how to make it happen not just some times but every time.

Take a look at the **Top Ten** "wants" of every airplane buyer.

1. **Mid-time engine**
2. **Lower airframe time than fleet average**
3. **No damage history**
4. **No hail marks**
5. **No corrosion**
6. **Complete log books since new**
7. **All ADs and SBs complied with**
8. **No repetitive ADs**
9. **No repetitive SB's**
10. **Never been a trainer**

Buy an airplane that violates **ANY** of these **Top Ten** and you **Will Absolutely** have trouble selling it. Eventually you will succeed but at a steep discount and with many sleepless nights beforehand.

As a seller you want to offer a product that everybody wants. When you do the market will expect to pay a higher than average price to own your bird.

Imagine that you are going to buy today and sell tomorrow not some day in the foggy future but tomorrow. This attitude will help you find *value* while others search for low price. The difference is simple. A good value is yours when you pay lower than market price for a highly desirable flying machine. If you buy it right then you can sell it effortlessly for a profit the day after you buy it. **Buy Low - Sell High** is **THE** winning business axiom for a reason. It is the basis of **ALL** profit.

Let's use the example of buying a trainer as that's where most owner/pilots get started with aircraft ownership. I know I did.

In the fall of 2013, **Trade-A-Plane** had 55 Cessna 150s listed for sale on their website. They ranged in price from $12,000 to $46,000 with an average asking price of $22,000.

Two questions spring to mind.

Is the one at $12,000 a bargain?

Is the guy asking $46,000 crazy?

Before you start scanning *aircraft for sale* ads in a serious way it is important to appreciate what you want to wind up with and to recognize the "cheapest" path to get you there. In most cases, a solid mid-time engine will top your *"must have"* list and it should.

Here's why. Air Power, Inc. (***www.airpowerinc.com***) will sell you a new Continental O200 (the C150's powerplant) for $28,000; a factory rebuilt one for $24,000 or a factory rebuild of your current engine for $20,000.

Buying a new or rebuilt engine is not something you ever want to do with a low dollar airplane. In the Cessna 150 purchase we are exploring, the cost of the engine exceeds the average asking price for the airplane. Buying a trainer that needs an engine is a bone headed move that can be easily avoided by hiring a qualified

IA to go through the engine logbook and the engine before you purchase the ship.

Other high dollar mistakes that aircraft buyers make are hidden in the panel and the buyer's aspirations for it.

There is nothing wrong with a panel that is made up of ancient flight instruments arranged in the *"wherever they'll fit"* manner of the 1960's and 1970's. That is, there is nothing wrong with it unless you **MUST** have modern flight instruments in a six-pack arrangement and would really prefer a glass display from Garmin or Aspen.

If you must have a glass panel, count on spending a minimum of $15,000. Settling for a modern style "steam gauge" upgrade and a modification of the panel to accommodate a "six pack" will easily empty $6,000 from your wallet.

The majority of used aircraft were manufactured in the 1960's and the 1970's as that was the hay day of aircraft manufacturing in the United States. Many of these airplanes have the same avionics they left the factory with. Some have been upgraded to newer King Silver Crown style digital equipment, a few will have a panel mounted and IFR certified GPS with a moving map display.

If you have a strong desire to fly behind at least a Garmin 430W and will settle for nothing less be prepared to spend big bucks. Consider that you can buy a used one for roughly $5,000 but it will cost another $1,500 to have it installed and integrated with your panel. To get full use of a 430W you will want to add the necessary equipment to display nearby traffic which will call for a semi-expensive transponder upgrade. The modification to add a fully functional 430W, the transponder it requires and a navigation indicator that can display its feeds will run you about $14,000 installed which is more than 50% of the asking price of the current crop of advertised used Cessna 150's.

Over the years as its paint wears thin more than the plane's appearance suffers. Thin paint can't fend off corrosion. If the Cessna 150 you are about to buy needs paint count on spending $8,000. Go with a good shop that will apply an anti-corrosion treatment before painting.

If the seats are ripped, the springs sprung, the carpets holey and the plastic panels cracked you will understandably lust for a new interior. An interior job for even a small aircraft like the Cessna 150 will cost $4,000. If it's also time for new windows and windshields add another $2,000.

How about the tires and brakes? These are not elective items, they are safety items. Brakes and tires will run you $1,500 installed.

At this point it would make sense to buy a new battery. You'll be glad you did. It'll set you back $150. Compared to everything else that's a bargain!

The point is clear, buying and upgrading an airplane is a really bad financial move. It is by far best to buy an airplane that is equipped as you desire and is currently in the condition you desire.

If you bought the cheapest Cessna 150 and applied all of the changes detailed above, here's what you'd be looking at:

1. **$12,000 Cessna 150**
2. **$20,000 Engine (rebuilding yours)**
3. **$6,000 New Steam Gauges**
4. **$12,000 Modern but Used Avionics**
5. **$8,000 Paint**
6. **$4,000 Interior**
7. **$2,000 Windows**
8. **$1,500 Brakes and tires**

TOTAL $65,500

You would then own a nicely equipped, good looking Cessna 150 for which you paid three times the asking price of the average 150 presently available. Clearly, the monetary cost is unreasonable.

Consider also that your airplane would be unavailable for flying for at least six months to have all of the upgrades and modifications applied.

Is it worth it?

Absolutely not?

The lesson is to look long and hard and be prepared to compromise on both the equipment you want and the price you'll pay. There are great airplanes out there, offered at fair prices but you have to look for them.

This is a game like horseshoes and hand grenades where close counts. Getting everything you want on a **USED** airplane likely won't happen but you must search until you get **CLOSE** enough to everything you want to pull the trigger. Buying a plane that needs a new interior is OK if it compensates you for the trouble and expense with something that wasn't even on your wish list like an autopilot.

One of the 55 Cessna 150's advertised on that fall day of 2013 would make any buyer happy if he was willing to pay more than the average asking price for much, much more than the average airplane. This would be a classic **VALUE** purchase!

Have a look:

1975 Cessna 150M, 6122 TT, 808 SMOH
Latest compressions as of April 9, 2013 - 75, 78, 76, 76
26 hours since prop overhaul

STEC 50 auto pilot with altitude hold
Garmin 340 audio panel
Garmin 430 WAAS GPS
Garmin 327 digital transponder
King KX-155 NAV/COM
Stormscope
Digital outside temperature
Digital volt meter
Custom installed low oil pressure warning light
Vertical card compass
Custom installed annunciator lights and switches for GPS,
Nav 1 and Nav 2 tracking for AP
Interior rated 9
Three tone custom interior - charcoal, dove gray, & red
Interior refurbished in 2011 including:
New Carpet
New Seatbelts
New Shoulder Harnesses
Plenty of New Plastic
Custom Placards
Rosen Visors
Seros Air Vents
Three tone custom paint - red, burgundy, & white
Paint rated 7 - 7.5
Wheel Pants
Good Tires
Long range fuel tanks
Wingtip strobes
Tail strobe
Tanis heater
Lord shimmy damper
Aircraft cover
Cowl plugs
Personalized chocks

That's a wonderfully equipped 150 that anyone would be pleased to own, me included.

The problem is the asking price.

At $36,500 it is 50% higher than the average C150 offered and three times the asking price of the cheapest one.

The price can be easily justified by knowing what you want to wind-up with. It is not possible to buy the $12,000 machine and upgrade it to this level for anything less than **TWICE** the $36,500 asking price.

Value trumps price.

Don't kid yourself into believing that you can upgrade with baby steps; adding a few upgrades each year won't save you a penny. It doesn't matter when you spend the money. Throw all of your receipts into a shoe box and add 'em up when you're done. If you ever finish the project, you will have spent well over $72,000 for a plane you could have bought and enjoyed years earlier for just $36,500.

What are the chances that you can ever get that $72,000 back or that you will keep and be satisfied flying a Cessna 150 forever?

Is there a market for a $72,000 Cessna 150?

NO!

When buying a used aircraft you have two ways to go. Find the plane that most closely matches your wish list and buy it without worrying too much about the price. The other possibility is to compromise on your wish list in order to pay the price you have in mind.

Your purchase will be dominated by either price or wish list. Choose the "wish list" path and enjoy your plane. Choose the "price" path and learn to deal with your airplane's shortcomings every time you fly it.

This doesn't mean that you shouldn't set a budget and get the very best deal on the very best airplane you can. It simply means that you must first understand what you want and appreciate what it should cost. If you can't get what you want at a price you can afford to pay it is best to call off the hounds and wait until you can line up some more cash. Buying a "cheap heap" will wind up costing you more than a value priced but more expensive airplane.

Eventually you must get what you want and find a way to pay for it. A long time after you've forgotten the price, you'll still be enjoying the plane that lives in your hangar.

Nicely update panel of an older Cessna 182 straight tail.

(A 6 pack modified panel is nice and a fairly affordable redo.)

Completed Cessna 182RG Panel after it was upgraded.

(This nicely modified panel is obtainable, at a high price in.)

The same Cessna 182RG panel as the redo job gets underway. Step one was to remove all of the old equipment.

(This job will get much worse before it gets better.)

**The same Cessna 182RG panel as the upgrade job progresses.
Some of the new wiring has already been strung.**

*(It is cheaper and easier to buy an airplane that has already gone
through the headache mill when somebody else owned it! You
really don't want to go through this.)*

Chapter II
The Right Plane

The BIG Idea: How to make a reality based "wish list".

In every pilot's DNA lurks the desire to own an airplane. That's the nature of pilots. Aircraft ownership is a lifelong journey that springs from a love of flying and flying machines. The moment one plane is purchased every pilot's attention shifts to finding its replacement. The airplane we buy today, though perfect for our current purpose, will one day be traded as our need changes. Eventually yesterday's passion must be abandoned to make way for tomorrow's promise. It is better to be a servant of the future than a slave of the past.

A dream can only become a reality when it is accompanied by an adequate budget; one that measures not only cash but also time, travel and effort. The budget goes much deeper than acquisition, operating and maintenance costs. The expense of finding, buying and one day selling the machine must be considered. Each discovery takes thought, time, effort and money. Before we can find what we are looking for we must know what we want and understand that there is no perfect airplane and certainly there is no "**one size fits all**" airplane.

Every flying machine begins life as a compromise. Drag, lift, speed and cost are the major components of the airplane design process. A high lift wing is also a high drag wing; conversely a high speed wing is also a low lift wing. An F-16 is not the best choice for operating out of a 1,800 foot long bumpy grass strip and a Super Cub is a poor solution for traveling at the speed of heat.

I quickly discovered renting was frustrating, especially so when trying to finish my PPL. Buying an airplane of my own seemed like the right way to go. My ship would be available when I could fly. No more standing in line. No more worrying about the true condition of the machine that I was entrusting with my life. In 1990, I purchased my first airplane.

Not any airplane would do and not the type of airplane I ultimately wanted; I needed a trainer for now not for always as training not traveling was my current mission.

There are many trainers I could have considered and a couple that I wish I had purchased instead of what I bought but I was anxious and too quickly narrowed my hunt to just two options. I have never made this *'hair trigger'* mistake again. Knowing all the possibilities before creating a short list is the only thing that makes sense.

My recent flight experience had been in both Cessna 150s and Piper Tomahawks. While I liked them both I favored the appearance of the Tomahawk. Armed with absolutely no technical knowledge that could support choosing one over the other I froze. Clearly I needed to uncover some empirical data that would lead me to the right decision.

I setup **a pre-purchase education budget**. One hundred and fifty dollars seemed about right. It bought the books, manuals and magazine article reprints I felt would bring me up to speed.

The most valuable information came from two great books by the same author. Bill Clarke's **The Cessna 150 & 152** as well as his **Piper Indians.** The later had a really good section on the Tomahawk.

I devoured every page of these books and still have them on a shelf in my office. They helped me learn all of the things about both ships that I never knew I never knew and explained the differences between models and years. Mr. Clarke commented on the maintenance trouble points to expect with each. The starter gear on the 150, for example, is fragile and can cost big bucks to replace. Treating it with care is the best path. The Tomahawk had an AD on its spar that was expensive and time consuming to deal with.

He addressed the flying characteristics and cabin comfort of each. Without doubt the Tomahawk is roomier and more comfortable for a student and instructor. On the other hand, the Tomahawk will easily drop a wing and roll into an unexpected spin during stall practice.

The 150 is a tight fit but is forgiving and can be flown with no surprises by even the most ham fisted pilot wanna' be.

After reading and re-reading these two books, I decided that the Cessna 150 was the best choice for me. The fleet was larger, parts were readily available, secondary vendors were plentiful and there was an active type club which I gladly and quickly joined. The fact that the resale market for 150s was strong and would likely remain so was the icing on the cake.

I reasoned that I could buy my trainer, use it to get my license, fly it for fun for a while and then sell it for at least as much as I had paid for it. I would be out the cost of consumables, insurance, tie down fees and maintenance. A quick calculation showed me that those costs divided by the number of hours I would fly beat the rental charges I was then paying by 50 percent!

Good deal?

No.

GREAT deal!

22,000 Cessna 150's rolled off the Wichita, Kansas assembly line during its 1959 to 1978 production run. Over that time span, the mighty 150 evolved just like the Volkswagen Beetle of the same time period.

Slight design changes came along as they were continually improved. Without doubt the newer ones are better machines than the older ones. In 1959 they had a straight tail, no rear window and an oddly shaped panel that couldn't begin to hold the avionics, flight and engine instruments that today's aviators demand.

The one thing all 150s have in common is the Continental O200 engine. The powerplant is the biggest difference between the Cessna 150 and its successor the Cessna 152 which sports the more economical and nearly bullet proof Lycoming O-320. Its TBO was stretched to 2,400 hours which bested the competition from Continental by 600 hours. That difference saves flight schools across America big bucks. It also accounts for a much higher market price for the 152. It's worth more so it cost more. Imagine that!

I clearly didn't intend to own my trainer long enough to benefit from the lower operating cost associated with the C-152 over the C-150. Hence my decision went quickly and correctly to the lower priced and for me higher valued C-150. My intentions were to fly it for no more than 150 hours and to own it for less than one year.

Of the three 150 models that were produced; Standard, Commuter and Aerobat, I leaned towards the Commuter. It came from the factory with wheel pants, steps and handles, more comfortable seats and a few other features that appealed to me and I assumed the person who would one day purchase it from me. The wheel pants improved its appearance and cruise performance. The steps and handles made it easy to reach the fuel tanks without having to carry a step ladder in the back of the plane.

I wanted the more modern swept tail rather than the old fashion straight tail. I also wanted the increased visibility afforded by the rear window. The new style panel that came on line in 1966 appealed to me. After weighing the pros and cons of each model and each year I decided that a 150 Commuter manufactured after 1966 and before 1972 would be my best choice.

"Ask the man who owns one"

That's the best advice any of us can take.

Type clubs are nothing more and nothing less than a group of pilots who band together to support, learn about and educate others on the issues regarding their favorite airplane. In those days, the **Cessna** 150/152 Club was operated by Skip Carden. He and his hard working wife put out a monthly newsletter which was filled with advice from fellow owners, display ads from parts vendors and a classified section where used 150s were bought and sold..

Type clubs ordinarily maintain a technical support hotline. It's the place to get all of your **"how do I"** and **"what's the best......."** questions answered. One of the more important features of type clubs is their recommendations of mechanics and flight instructors plus their up-to-date list of ADs and SBs. Study these closely. They can lead you away from a budget buster. The many discussions I had with the technical support volunteers at the **Cessna 150/1522 Club** lead me to narrow my search to the 1967 150G.

The most important use of a type club is to connect with local owner/pilots of the aircraft you are researching. Contact the ones that have the year and model you are interested in and get together for lunch. "Hangar fly" with these guys. What do they like, what do they hate?

Ask if you can make a $100 Hamburger run together. Make it clear that you will buy the fuel and the burger. Few pilots can refuse an offer of free food and fuel. During the flight ask if you can take the controls. Fly with as many local guys as you can. Most of the planes of the same type fly the same way. Certainly some airplanes of the same type will fly differently due to the airframe modifications the owner may have made. Forget the manners of the modified machines and focus on the straight from the factory examples. Do you like the way these ships fly? If not, now is the time to make another decision.

That is exactly what I did with Mooney aircraft later in my flying career. They are wonderful ships for many people. Mooneys are faster than fast for the power they have been designed to carry.

I don't like the pilot's seating position. I know what the benefit of that design is; I just don't find it comfortable on long cross-countries. Many others do!

Mooney's can eat up a lot of runway when landing. They "float". If you get setup wrong or land long the safest thing to do is abort and go around. Al Mooney was a brilliant guy and there are legions of pilots who sincerely love his machine. My first look was at an M20E. I later considered an M20J. They are wonderful airplanes for somebody else.

The remainder of my $150 pre-purchase education fund was spent on reprints of magazine reviews of the Cessna 150, a **Cessna Model 150 Owner's Manual - 1967** and a subscription to **Trade-A-Plane.**

In the days before the internet the place to go for listings of planes for sale was certainly **Trade-A-Plane**. It came out three times a month. **Trade-A-Plane** is still out there and still serves a vital role. Today it has many challengers. The main advantage of **Trade-A-Plane** then and now is its help in understanding the value of the purchase you are considering by allowing a comparison of current alternatives.

Fortunately, pre-purchase education funds can be better spent today than when I bought my 150. The process is the same but there are more choices and the speed of delivery is instantaneous thanks to the internet. The biggest change for me is the ability to do more comparison shopping.

You'll be amazed at how much information is available on every machine by doing a simple Google search.

The best gift of the internet is what it has done for type clubs. Today each has multiple discussion areas setup for covering every aspect of owning their type. This is the best place to get an immediate recommendation for a mechanic, who specializes in caring for your kinda' bird, and lives in your area.

I belong to several type clubs and often ask competitive questions when considering my next aircraft. There is no better place to learn about the weak points of a Cessna Corvalis than to ask about it on the COPA (Cirrus Owner Pilot Association) website site. Ask the guys on the ABS (American Bonanza Society) website how a Cessna 210 compares with an A36 Bonanza. They'll be glad to fill you in.

Then go to the CPA (Cessna Pilots Association) website (*www.cessna.org*) and ask the same question in reverse. Appendix A of this book has a list of type clubs and websites that you'll find useful. Most demand that you become a dues paying member before they give you access or help, others are free and some straddle the line by offering a no cost trial membership.

The first question you must ask the type club representing the aircraft you have interest in is for a list of AD's and SB's. Review it carefully. Some will be show stoppers for you. Others will merely cause you to make certain that the AD or SB has been complied with and in the case of a repetitive AD or AB has been continually adhered to. ADs and SBs can be expensive. Make certain that any airplane you consider buying documents compliance with ALL ADs and SBs.

Finding helpful books is a snap, go to Amazon.Com type in the name of the plane you want to read about and you'll be presented with several choices that will fill the bill. Pick one or more and stand by your mailbox. They'll show up in about two days.

Magazine reviews are even easier. Go to one of the aviation oriented magazines and see if they have **EVER** published a review on your machine. They have, they all have. It may have been several years ago which doesn't matter as the article will likely come from the same era as the plane you're researching. Appendix B of this book list the websites all of the magazines you'll want to contact.

Keep a notebook and pen at your side as you study, make a lot of notes; they'll come in handy when you start the search for the plane you are about to buy. Once you've decided on the plane, model and year that you want; make a list of all of my **MUST HAVE, NICE TO HAVE** and **PLUS** features. On the same page list all of your **NO WAY** issues.

Have a heart-to-heart meeting with yourself to get to the bottom of what you are willing to accept and where you draw the line.

Here are a few that will get you started:

1. **Will I buy only from the owner?**
2. **Would a low-time airframe please or scare me?**
3. **Will I only purchase a NO DAMAGE aircraft?**
4. **What about hail damage?**
5. **What about hangar rash?**
6. **Must the aircraft have been hangared?**
7. **What about a history of or present evidence of corrosion?**
8. **Must all of the log books from birth forward be present and in good order?**
9. **On a 1 to 10 scale what must the condition of the paint be?**
10. **On a 1 to 10 scale what must the condition of the interior be?**
11. **Must all of the windows be excellent?**
12. **Are current photographs of the aircraft available?**

13. Will the owner provide copies of all logbooks?
14. Must the aircraft currently be in annual?
15. Are all AD's and SB's up to date?
16. What is the highest SMOH I would accept?
17. How long ago can the overhaul have been?
18. What total engine time is too high for me?
19. What are the lowest cylinder compressions I will consider?
20. What is the highest time I will accept on the prop?
21. What avionics must I have?
22. How much will I budget to upgrade the avionics?
23. What flight instruments must I have?

Each of these questions must be considered at some point. The best time is before you start looking at airplanes and talking to owners. Let's explore a few of them starting with # 1.

1. "Will I only buy from the owner?"

Only the owner can provide you with all of the information concerning his airplane and his use of it. No broker can fill that bill. Some brokers will put you in direct contact with the owner or pass your questions to him and his answers back to you. The second point is price. The owner is paying the broker out of your pocket as the broker cannot be expected to work for free. Saving the commission dollars in the case of a broker or the markup in the case of a dealer is by far the most economical way to go. I can think of many positive reasons to deal directly with the owner and no negative ones.

2. "Would a low-time airframe please or scare me?"

This question opens up the door to some very important questions about the care and feeding of an airplane. Every now and then I'll spot an ad for an airplane that was produced in the '60s and has less than a thousand hours on the airframe and engine. Is this the find of the century? The seller's ad will try to lead you to that conclusion.

Doesn't "low-time" really mean "hangar queen"? Isn't a "hangar queen" going to be a troubled airplane? The answer to both questions is yes unless the airplane in question was "pickled"; not just the engine but the entire airplane.

To remain in good condition an airplane like a racehorse needs to be exercised regularly. If not, vital engine components develop pitting, and the airframe becomes the home to a family of field mice, a hive of hornets and a bird's nest or two.

Airplanes should be flown at least 100 hours a year to stay in good shape. Those 100 hours should be evenly earned throughout the year. A plane that's been flown two hours a week is a plane you want to own.

What about a plane that's flown 1,000 hours over the last fifty years? That's 20 hours a year on average or 23 minutes a week if spread out evenly over the year.

Personally I'd much rather own a high-time airplane than a low-time one. Let's say that same fifty year old airplane has 10,000 hours on it. That works out to just 200 hours a year or four hours a week. That's hardly a number that implies this machine has been over worked and needs to be sent to the scrap heap but it surely means that it has been touched, flown and maintained regularily over the years.

A plane that is flown four hours a week is under the constant scrutiny of its pilot during pre and post flight inspections. It's a plane that is seeing an A&P on a regular basis. Nothing goes unnoticed with a high-time machine. A "hangar queen" on the other hand is invisible.

17. "How long ago can the overhaul have been?"

The average engine is rated at being capable of being used for 2,000 hours between overhauls. The engine will reach TBO out of the factory crate or off the rebuilder's bench if it is flown regularly and maintained properly. Simple! A plane flown 200 hours a year that has its oil changed every 25 hours has a great likelihood of meeting TBO.

A plane flown just 100 hours a year is less likely to see TBO. It can make it but it will undergo at least one TOP and maybe two. By the time it gets to TBO the crank and CAM will need to be sent away for servicing. Likely one or both of them will need to be replaced.

Ten years brings the 200 hour a year machine to TBO and a visit to the rebuild shop. If it's been ten years SMOH and only 1,000 hours have been logged it will need a TOP sooner rather than later even if it can currently satisfy a compression test. What if it's been twenty years and only 500 hours have been logged? The answer is easy. The new owner will soon be dealing with big engine maintenance issues. If it has been several years since the last overhaul, the engine is operating on borrowed time.

21. "What avionics must I have?"

When you buy an airplane that costs less than $100,000, the airframe is basically **FREE**. The value of the machine is the engine, the avionics, the paint job and the interior.

In the fall of 2013 the median asking price for a Cessna 150 stood at $22,000. The list price of a brand new 0-200 from TCM its manufacturer stood at $28,000 and change. That's after the exchange of a serviceable core *(your old engine)* for which they allow you $11,000. The actual list price of the engine without a core exchange is $38,749. It is possible to save a few bucks by buying a factory rebuilt engine. Its exchange price comes to $23,485 when purchased through Air Power, Inc. Crating, shipping, de-installing and installing charges must be added to the total cost of any engine replacement. Together these costs will add $3,000 to your shop bill.

Think of it this way. If someone gave you a used Cessna 150 for **FREE** on the condition that you **MUST** purchase a factory new engine for it, the cost of the engine would exceed the market value of the airplane.

A panel upgrade works out similarly. It is not possible to purchase a used Cessna 150 with old radios and outdated flight instruments and upgrade them to modern standards without losing a ton of cash plus enduring the aggravation of working with the shop to get the upgrade done.

The lesson is simple, buy an airplane that already has what you want or at least what you can live with.

If your objective is to have exactly what you want then buy whatever airplane suits you and begin the multiyear process of having it brought up to spec. The cost in time and money will be high but at the end of the day you'll have exactly what you want until you crave something else which is going to happen sooner than you imagine. You will lose a ton of time and money.

Chapter III

Sellers – Your Private List

The BIG Idea: To get the **best** deal on the **best** plane work exclusively with sellers that other buyers aren't aware of.

A successful purchase begins with a thoughtful pre-purchase strategy and the budget to carry it out. If your search turns up the perfect airplane in Seattle and you live in Miami the costs of kicking the tires may be too high to consider purchasing it.

Spending $1,000 merely to see and touch a particular Cessna 150 that can be purchased for $18,000 makes no sense. On the other hand, if you're about to buy a two year old Cirrus SR-22T, $1,000 is a small drop in a very large bucket. Basically, the higher the purchase price of the machine the more you can budget to check it out.

The pre-purchase budget isn't just about money though. Like the pre-purchase education budget; time, distance and effort must be taken into account. How far will you go to see a candidate and how much can you afford to spend to make that trip? Chances are very good that you will examine several planes before you buy one.

The cost of the search can be reined in by controlling the geography. G650 buyers need to cast a worldwide net. Cessna 172 hunters can find worthy candidates within 300 miles of their front porch. All of the online aircraft for sale websites offer a sort feature which will allow you to look at only the airplanes within the state you select.

You absolutely **MUST** use these sites and print off a list of **EVERYTHING** that is for sale on them. This will give you a great overview of current market conditions. How many planes of the type you are looking for are for sale and at what asking price? How far will you have to go to get a good one?

We all know that the **BEST** jobs are never advertised. The same thing is true when it comes to buying airplanes or houses or boats or anything else. The best deals aren't advertised.

Why?

It is because the owner isn't currently thinking about selling his machine. Maybe it's because he doesn't want to sell. Maybe it's because he wants to sell but doesn't think he can. Maybe it's because he never even thinks about his airplane.

To understand just how many airplanes **MIGHT** be for sale just visit any airport and notice how few hangar doors are ever opened and how few airplanes ever fly. Find a man that never uses or seldom even sees his airplane and ask him this simple question, *"Would you consider selling your airplane to me?"*

Here's a simple money saving game changer. To get the best deal on the best plane, increase the number of possibilities and work **EXCLUSIVELY** with sellers who aren't currently thinking of selling and aren't talking to other buyers.

Years ago, I accepted an assignment to turnaround a software company located in Munich, Germany. The list of issues confronting this company was long and the patience of the investors was short. It took about a year to get everybody happy and playing nice with each other again. The investors got every penny of their money back and a small profit to boot. Most of the employees kept their jobs. All of the customers' needs were met and they continued to buy. I was exhausted on the happy day I boarded a Delta jet to return to the United States at the end of this assignment. For the year or so that I worked this project I did not fly a private airplane and had sold mine before I left for Germany.

I wanted a plane again and I knew just what I wanted. A 'play' plane was what I had my heart set on. Not something to go anyplace in a hurry and not a trainer to begin my Commercial rating with. What I wanted was an early morning, late afternoon smooth air machine. Something to fly low and slow. A plane to chase Burgers was all that I was after.

The word Ercoupe entered my head and I couldn't get rid of it. It must have had something to do with the 'Coupes rear window which mirrors that of older VWs. Maybe I had adopted some German taste.

I grabbed a copy of **This & That about the Ercoupe** by Paul Prentice. The Ercoupe bug that had merely bitten me prior to reading Paul's wonderful book now had me in a bear hug. I quickly joined the **Ercoupe Owners' Club** and began my hunt for a machine. Anxiously I waited for the first issue of my renewed subscription to **Trade-A-Plane**. There I found just three 'Coupes listed for sale. That was it, just three, and they all looked like fugitives from the boneyard. Next I haunted my friends. That turned up one very tired basket case.

Then an idea came to me!

I contacted the FAA and bought a disk with their entire database of registered aircraft on it. Thankfully it was Excel formatted. That's how they did it in the mid-nineties. Today it's much easier. You can do it all at the FAA's website.

What you wind up with is a mailing list of all of the folks in your state who own the type of aircraft you're interested in. Compare it to the planes advertised for sale that you compiled earlier and strip those out of the FAA mailing list. The goal is to be the only buyer in your potential sellers' field of vision.

The next step is to send 'em a letter with a self-addressed stamped envelope inside. The letter I used to buy the Ercoupe I wanted was simple and effective. Here it is:

Johnny Owner
123 Elm Street
Lincoln, Il 12345

Dear Mr. Owner,

Within the next 30 days, I will be purchasing an Ercoupe. I am not an aircraft broker or an aircraft dealer, this airplane is for my personal use only. I intend to fly it and have no interest in reselling it.

The FAA records indicate that you own Ercoupe, N98115. It appears to match my needs.

Should you have interest in selling your airplane to me, please take a moment to call me at 555-222-1234. If you would prefer for me to call you, simply write your name and phone number on a piece of paper and drop it inside the self-addressed stamped envelope I have provided with this letter and I will call you the moment it reaches my mailbox. In any event, thanks very much for considering my interest in buying N98115.

Sincerely,

John Purner

PS
If you have no interest in selling your Ercoupe at this time but know someone else who might be interested in selling their Ercoupe. I would be very grateful if you passed along their name and phone number to me or my name and phone number to them.

The FAA list I was working with showed 97 Ercoupes based in the state of Texas, I sent this letter to the owner of each one of them. Six were returned with *"undeliverable address"* stamped across their face.

Eight owners called me; three more used the return envelope. Suddenly I had the names and telephone numbers of four times as many Ercoupes as **Trade-A-Plane** had and all of mine were in Texas! I could drive to them. One was in El Paso, 750 miles away! The others were all within 200 miles of my home.

My first phone call with each owner was carefully scripted.

This is a practice I still follow.

Here's what I say.

First, I thank them for responding to my letter. It pays to be polite and I really am grateful.

All of my initial questions are open ended. I want to hear what the owner has to say about himself and his airplane.

"How long have you been flying?"

Hopefully he'll open up and share a bit about himself. Before I buy an airplane I buy the man selling it. Buying a used anything is a game of "who do you trust". There are no guarantees and there are no warranties. If I am not comfortable with the seller then I won't buy from him. **You can't make a good deal with a bad person.**

As he speaks, I want to hear him profess a love of flying that has been with him since he was a child.

When does he fly, where does he fly, how often does he fly? Those are the questions I want answered but will not ask. Specific questions tend to lead the seller to an answer he can easily predict I want to hear. Open-ended questions allow him to ramble and tell me what's in his heart. If he loves flying and loves this airplane then chances are very good that he has "babied" it.

"Tell me about your airplane."

As he speaks, I listen intently and am contented to learn and take a few notes. Does he tell me when he bought the airplane and a bit of its prior history? Does he tell me how long he's owned it? Does he ramble on about its condition? Does he spew an endless list of technical details about this machine? Does he tell me where he has flown it and how much he has loved flying it? Why did he buy this aircraft, was it a good purchase, has he enjoyed owning it, does he fly it regularly? How many airplanes did he own before he bought this one?

The man I want to buy from sings the praises of what this airplane does and how it has made his life better not what it is made of. The technical details can all be found in the logbooks.

Buy an airplane only from a man who is in love with his airplane. We tend to take care of the things we love!

"If I buy your airplane, will you stop flying?"

The touchiest question of all is this one. It is really asking, "Why would you consider selling this airplane?" I don't want him to have seller's remorse just before we close the deal because he never considered what he would do without this airplane. Likewise, I don't want to learn that he stopped flying this airplane six years ago because he learned to hate it.

He might say that he'll stop flying because he's worried about his medical.

He might say he'll buy another one just like this one. That's a red flag, isn't it?

If he says he plans to keep flying but he isn't sure what, I have to wonder. Buying a bigger, faster or a smaller slower airplane is a good answer. Saying he is going to buy a share of his best friend's airplane is a good answer. Many answers are good answers. I just want to know what he's thinking. Then I can judge if his reason makes sense to me.

Before I hang-up I'll thank him for his time and let him know that I am interested in his airplane. I'll then ask if he could please send some current pictures and copies of the log books. **Notice that I have not mentioned price.**

Often the prospective seller will say something like, "How much are you intending to pay for my airplane?" I always answer with these words, "Exactly what it is worth, not a penny less and not a penny more. The package I've asked you to send me will help me understand your aircraft's true value. By the way, an equipment list would be helpful; could you please include one with the other items?"

A telephone call will be made to every person who responded and no airplane will be excluded during this first round of calls. The calls' true purpose is to move each potential seller to the next step. Causing them to go to the trouble to take some pictures and have them mailed or emailed, then to make copies of all of the logs and prepare and print an equipment list brings them to the realization that they are about to sell their airplane and to make up their minds that they truly want to.

Fanning the fires in a seller's oven is similar to setting the hook in the mouth of the brook trout you've been stalking on your favorite stream. You can't catch a fish until the hook is set and you can't buy an airplane until the current owner decides to sell.

Most of the respondents will follow through. Stand by your mailbox. Place a courteous reminder call to those who fail to stay in touch. "Hi Bill, this is John. Are you still interested in selling your airplane?" It's this second effort that brings the right plane at the right price.

Chapter IV

First Look

The BIG Idea: How to check out several airplanes for the price of one.

"Das Beste oder nichts" (English: "**The Best or Nothing**").

That's Mercedes-Benz new advertising slogan. It has been their marching order since inception. "The Best or Nothing" is also a great way to approach buying a used airplane. What's the value of a "hangar queen", a "rust bucket" or a "handyman Special"?

A low price doesn't mean that you got a great deal. It may mean that you overpaid. When I was in high school I bought a used VW bug for $1000. That was certainly a low price. The trouble was that the car was really worth about $200.

I live in Florida but have never and will never buy a plane that has spent most of its life here. No part of this state is further than 70 miles from the ocean. Simply stated, Florida is corrosion's first cousin. I buy only dry country airplanes – period, paragraph end of report.

That means that all of the solicitation letters I send out go to owner/pilots who live about 1,000 miles away.

Bummer!

While dry country airplanes are better, it can cost an arm and a leg to kick their tires. It isn't possible to make those costs go away but they can certainly be reduced.

Let's presume for a moment that the airplanes you have identified are all in Texas and that Texas is 1,000 miles away from your home base. First, decide what's to be accomplished during the "first look". It is a pretty important list.

Here's my suggestion:

1. **Is the aircraft airworthy?**
2. **Does the ship match the logs and the photos?**
3. **Does it appear to be clean and well cared for?**
4. **Are the windows clear with no crazing or cracks?**
5. **Does it have any corrosion?**
6. **Is the interior serviceable without cuts or tears?**
7. **Is it equipped with shoulder harnesses?**
8. **Does it have all of the listed equipment?**
9. **Is the belly coated with oil?**
10. **Is the engine clean?**
11. **What's the appearance of the engine oil?**
12. **How much oil is in the engine?**
13. **Is the prop free of nicks and dings?**
14. **Are the tires serviceable?**
15. **Is the landing gear in good condition?**
16. **Do all of the avionics work properly?**
17. **Do all of the flight instruments work properly?**
18. **Do the fuel gauges read correctly?**
19. **Do the flaps function properly?**
20. **Does the electrical system function properly?**
21. **Does the engine start easily?**
22. **Does it idle smoothly at low RPM?**
23. **Do all engine instruments indicate proper operation?**
24. **Do the brakes function properly?**
25. **Do the magnetos pass the run-up test?**
26. **If the aircraft is equipped with a constant speed propeller does it test properly?**

This is an easy list to go through given a couple of hours. Any self-respecting pilot could do these inspections himself except for item #1 and item #5. The airworthiness check, Item #1, is the magic of our "first look" strategy. You will be inviting each owner to fly his plane a reasonable distance to an inspection point you will pre-arrange in his home state. **The goal is to use only one inspection point for ALL of the airplanes you're considering and to have the sellers come to you.**

If the owner is willing to strap into his machine and fly it on a short cross country you know that he is willing to trust his life to this airplane. He at least considers it to be airworthy and he knows more about the condition of the airplane than you do.

What if he refuses and says "No! You can inspect it at my airport. I won't come to you." Thank the gentleman for his time and scratch him off the list. He's either arrogant or afraid. You don't want to own a plane that the previous owner was unwilling to fly even when someone else is willing to pay for his fuel. Yes, part of the strategy is for you to pay for the fuel.

I'll bet that all of us would fly more often if someone else offered to pay for our fuel. You also don't want the unpleasant experience of trying to negotiate with someone who refuses to meet you half way on this easy issue. You're flying 1,000 miles and are asking him to fly less than 100.

For a state the size of Texas I sometimes have to use two inspection points. The goal is for no owner to fly for more than one hour to the inspection point. Your job is to contract with a local A&P who will allow you to use his ramp to meet your sellers and inspect their planes. You will pay him to do a corrosion inspection on each plane. That gives you a temporary home and takes care of #5 the corrosion inspection. With careful planning you can squeeze in three planes a day.

The type clubs are the best place to go for a list of A&Ps who specialize in the type aircraft you are focused on.

You must offer to pay for the owner's fuel *to and from* the inspection point. Again, most will take you up on your offer because they like to fly and trust their airplanes. You really do have to wonder about the ones who won't fly even on your nickel. Do they not like to fly or do they have concerns about their airplane or are they simply hard to get along with? Whatever the reason, some sellers will fall away at this point. That's good as it tightens your focus and lowers your cost. By the time this "first look" inspection actually happens, your twelve plane target list will have fallen to six.

The corrosion inspection should cost about $75 per airplane. That $450 total for the six aircraft is some of the best money you will ever spend. It will exclude aircraft that have serious corrosion issues that the current owner likely wasn't aware of. Sometimes it helps spot an issue that the current owner didn't want you to find. Corrosion is something that A&Ps are trained to spot. They know where to look and they know what represents a high dollar problem and what is a quick fix.

A new paint job is like lipstick on a pig. It is often used to cover problems that a prospective owner would run from if he could see them. That's another reason to buy from a list of owners that you developed rather than buying from a broker or dealer. Very few of your guys were trying to sell before your contact. Typically you won't be presented with an airplane with a new paint job that an owner is using to cover up damage or corrosion. Rarely will the A&P find corrosion so severe that the aircraft involved will be deemed unsafe to fly.

What about the cost of all that fuel you've promised to buy? In the worst case that comes to three hours of fuel for each ship. One hour down, one hour back and one hour for the test flight you'll be conducting. The average big bore single uses 16 gallons an hour as the burn rate. It's best to round the total up to fifty gallons per airplane. Using a fuel price of five bucks a gallon you'll be handing each owner a check for $250. The total cost of this "first look" inspection trip comes to $2,500 including the flight over, lodging and meals.

A successful "first look" requires some planning and three pieces of equipment. An iPAD is really a requirement, to record the test flight data and to verify the aircrafts' flight and navigation equipment during the test flights. There are several software apps available for you to choose from if you haven't already. Be certain, that the one you use provides flight planning, GPS navigation, flight instrument simulation and flight logging. It is best to use the same flight plan for all of the test flights. That helps you compare apples-to-apples when you're back home reviewing the "first look" data.

Photography is the best memory refreshing technique known to man. If you don't have one of the new digital SLR cameras that double as video recorders, get one! They allow you to take some wonderful still shots of the airplanes you'll be inspecting and capture some great video of it in flight and the current owner and the A&P with it.

When you get home a look at a video of the A&P pointing out the various corrosion points on a particular aircraft will be very helpful. It will also be refreshing to look at the video you took of the owner landing at the inspection airport and taxiing up to the maintenance hangar.

I take stills of every point on the airplane and do a narrated video walk around of each plane pointing out the important items; the good, the bad and the ugly! Remembering the details of six planes is not possible without some strong reminders.

I review all the videos with my hometown A&P to get his opinion. It's a cheap way to bring him along.

The flight test is the most important aspect of your inspection. You need two ways to record it. One is the flight log from the iPAD. The second is an in-cockpit video complete with intercom and nav/com radio audio. Buy a **GoPro Hero3** video camera and the headset attachment that goes with it. Installing it prior to each test flight takes about thirty seconds. Position it behind and over the pilot's left shoulder using its suction cup mount. Focus the camera on the panel so the flight instruments and avionics are all visible. Narrate the test flight over the intercom, the Hero3 will create an amazing video which you should download to your computer at the conclusion of each test flight.

The test flights' run-up should be done with more care than normal. Taking notes and narrating the Hero3 video during the run-up is critical for there is little chance of remembering the details of six run-ups and six test flights. If anything shows up during the pre-flight or the run-up, **do not** fly the plane, instead taxi back to the hangar, shut the engine down and let the owner deal with the problem.

Two options are presented to him. He can arrange for your host A&P to fix the squawk or he can simply shake hands and say good-bye. If the fix can be accomplished before you leave re-do the test flight, if not merely scratch this aircraft from your list.

Assuming there are no major run-up issues, prepare for takeoff. Your goal is to climb to 5,000 feet AGL using the Best Rate of Climb power setting from the POH. Once there, change to the cruise power and prop settings, trim the ship and see how she flies hands off. Compare the indicated airspeed to the one in the POH for this altitude, temperature and air pressure.

Now it's time to do a couple of maneuvers. Start with a 30 degree bank into a 360 degree turn to the left followed by the same maneuver to the right noticing how willing she is to hold altitude. Next, trim for slow flight and again go hands off. If all is well to this point do a gentle power off stall. While doing these simple maneuvers constantly check the flight and engine instruments. Paying particular attention to oil temp, oil pressure and alternator output.

The best test of the navigation system is to fly the flight plan you prepared. It should include a triangular route from the inspection airport to two other airports or intersections if you prefer. The iPAD software you use must have an excellent flight logging feature. Once you're back on the ground, you can replay the entire flight to understand and compare the performance of the various aircraft; rate of climb for example and the precision of the route you flew.

The goal during the flight is to verify all of the flight instruments, engine instruments and avionics. Does everything function? Are their indications believable? The navigation equipment's readings can be compared with the iPAD during the flight. The same is true for some of the flight instruments.

When the flight is over, taxi back to the maintenance hangar and perform some simple post flight inspections. The first two are easy and obvious. Check the oil for color and quantity. Take an oil sample from the sump to be sent away for an oil analysis. Then crawl under the airplane to check the belly, and the bottom of the wings. You're looking for any fluid leaks; fuel, oil or hydraulics.

Finally, bid farewell to the owner and make some post "first look" inspection notes. What was your overall impression? What did the A&P think and what if anything did he find? Your most important writing covers the flight. Did you enjoy flying this airplane or was it a struggle? What did you wish it had that it doesn't? Did everything work?

Planes of the same type often fly very differently. The takeoff and initial climb reveal much about the true condition of the engine. The simple flight maneuvers will tell you everything you need to know about the tuning of the airplane and the flight controls. Did the wings remain level when you did the power off stall or did it drop a wing? If you suddenly owned this airplane would you be comfortable with it exactly as it is or would you want to make some immediate panel, airframe or engine changes? Is there anything that raised a flag about this airplane?

Soon the "first look" trip will end and you'll be on your way back home. You now know two or three planes that you would like to own and you know two or three that you don't want. Your subconscious has ranked the planes for you. For whatever reason, you are drawn to one more than the others. It is your target. The herd has been culled.

What about price?

What about value?

What about the offer?

Chapter V

How was it flown? - The 4th Log Book

The Big Idea: The owner's log book tells every airplanes true story.

You kicked the tires and studied some great airplanes. The A&P you used weighed in with some things to consider and somehow you're drawn to a certain plane. You now know everything about it except for the most important things.

Who really flew this plane?

How has it been used?

The airframe, engine and propeller logs don't give you this information. They certainly let you know how many hours it has been flown and how it's been maintained over the years but they reveal nothing about who flew it and what sort of missions it went on?

Buying a used aircraft involves reading. You'll wade through a ream of ancient magazine articles and flight reviews as you narrow your hunt for the perfect bird. Is a Bonanza better than a Husky? Depends on your mission I suppose. Hauling 5 people is not something a Husky can do. On the other hand, landing on the side of a mountain in less than 800 feet is a great way to bend your Bo. If somebody gave you an Ercoupe would you want it? I would, by the way, you might not. Choosing the perfect aircraft type is a lot like choosing the perfect ice cream. **There is no right answer, only personal preference.**

The day has come when you've narrowed the field down to one airplane. Now the hard work and the serious reading begin. Long before the pre-purchase inspection you'll want to study the log books one more time. All of them! For a single engine airplane that means four. Let's add 'em up:

Air Frame Log

Engine Log
Propeller Log
Pilot's Log

The first three are pretty standard and everyone knows what to look for in them. **Most of us never think about the fourth log book and it is the most important one of all.** Here's why. Knowing who's been flying this machine, for what purpose and in what manner answers many questions that aren't addressed in the other three logs.

Several years ago I decided that I needed a machine that sucked up its gear. My choice was a Piper Arrow as I was a Piper guy in those days. The one I fancied had just celebrated its twenty-fifth birthday. The current owner indicated that he had purchased the machine ten years earlier and was the third owner. The log books supported his contention.

No obvious problems cropped up in the engine, airframe or prop log books. They all matched perfectly and all agreed that this airplane had been flown about 100 hours every year. That corresponded perfectly with the owner's statement that the airplane was flown for the personal transportation of his family only and had never been used for flight training. When I asked to see his **Pilot Log Book** he resisted but turned it over when my interest in his ship cooled.

You can put a hundred hours a year on an airplane in many different ways. Some are good for the airplane and some will lead to future problems. The ideal hundred hours a year airplane is flown once a week on a flight of approximately one hour out and one hour back – the perfect Burger Run. An hour flight gives the engine plenty of time to heat up and burn off any contaminants in the oil. That's critically important. Longer flights give the pilot time to observe the plane and all of its systems in cruise at a set altitude. Finally the plane will experience only two landings. The descents can be well managed to avoid shock cooling.

If two hours a week is best, what's worst? One hundred one hour flights all spent in the pattern.

Here's why. The engine never gets hot enough to burn off the crud that hides in dirty oil and the engine is constantly shock cooled as the pilot climbs at full throttle to pattern altitude, then pulls the power to set up for the next landing. Pattern work and touch and go landings are tough on all aircraft systems. Everything in the panel gets shaken during each landing. An airplane that never left the pattern is not an airplane you want to own. Neither is an airplane that has been flown less than 100 hours a year. That's the minimum you should consider. A two hundred hours a year airplane is best. Again, if the hours are used flying not pattern dancing.

The Pilot Log book of the Arrow's owner proved that it wasn't a pattern patroller. It definitely went on long trips. That's all it did!

For the past ten years the plane was flown from central Missouri to the Bahamas in the winter and central Missouri to Canada in the summer. The rest of the year it sat in the hangar. The owner was a fisherman; ocean, lake and stream. He chased bonefish across the Bahamas and trout across Canada. I was jealous of his lifestyle but surely didn't want his plane.

An engine gets really dry during six months of inactivity. After two months, the cylinder walls are totally unprotected, corrosion begins, pitting results. Four months later some cowboy twists the starter key. The piston rings rub against those pitted cylinder walls; compressions fall from the mid-70s to the mid-60s as this once proud engine becomes an oil burner. What about the camshaft and the crankshaft? The story is the same. Engine parts that aren't protected by oil corrode when idle then wear when used.

Imagine for a moment that the owner's logbook revealed that he never flew this airplane or flew it very little. The airplane logs show that it has been doing some flying and the pilot's log book show that he isn't the guy that flew it. This makes the purchase referees drop yellow flags all over this purchase decision.

Why hasn't he flown this airplane?

Who has? One pilot or many?

How has it been used?

Why haven't any of those guys bought it?

Why does the owner possess a flying machine that he never uses?

Does he fly another airplane?

What kind of airplane?

If it is this machine's cousin you should have a million question that all lead to one answer. This airplane isn't for you.

The usage reported in the Airframe, Engine and Propeller logs can't tell an airplane's complete story. The **Pilot's Log** fills in the blanks. Never buy a plane until you've read the owner's log. If he won't show it to you, don't buy his plane.

Chapter VI

The Art of the Offer

The BIG Idea: A good deal is a fair deal.

Finally, you've found **THE** airplane. It's been a long journey; you've worked hard and spent some money on the search. Now you're going to spend considerably more to make this dream machine yours. That's what the buying journey has been all about. The time has come to make an offer.

What price is the current owner willing to accept? In addition to setting the price you'll need to agree on some other conditions that affect the transfer. If all goes well, he'll pass you the keys and you'll hand him a basketful of cash. That's a win-win!

The price of an airplane is any number that the buyer is willing to pay and the seller is willing to accept. The **value** of the plane is something entirely different. It is what the plane is now worth on the open market in its current condition. If that's true and it is, then it makes sense to **know the value before trying to set the price.**

If both parties are to walk away as winners then the **price** must exactly reflect the **value**. The buyer should pay exactly one dollar for something that is valued at exactly one dollar. Likewise the seller should receive a dollar for a dollar's value.

Step one is to visit again all of the aircraft for sale websites and pull up all of the planes that match the one you're about to buy. Discerning the median price is easy.

The advertisements listing aircraft for sale will only tell you what the current asking price is for each airplane offered. You might think the offering prices are too high and the seller might think they're too low but you must both agree that these **are** the current asking prices.

Be certain to match up the feature list of the planes advertised with the equipment list of the airplane you are interested in buying.

Adjust the price accordingly, up or down. No two used airplanes will be identical. The avionics will be different; the airframe hours will be different; the time since major overhaul will be different accordingly the price must be adjusted.

Right?

No, it is absolutely - **Wrong!**

That's the wonderful thing about averages they take everything into consideration. The median price is the median price. It is an also an asking price not a selling price.

Is it possible to learn the selling prices of all the aircraft of this type? How about a few? How about any?

The short answer is **no**.

Aircraft selling prices unlike home selling prices are not recorded. Aircraft selling prices are not a matter of public record. There are companies that claim to have these figures but they truly don't. What they have is a database of selling prices that have been reported to them on a voluntary basis by anyone who has recently sold an aircraft. Very few if any individuals report. Largely the data collected comes from brokers and dealers. How reliable do you suppose that information is?

At the end of the day the only trustworthy information you can have is the median asking price; that and only that. The dilemma remains; what should you offer?

How much should you pay?

What is the **value**?

The median asking price is actually the "ceiling" price. The median asking price establishes the highest price you should pay for this machine as it is the price at which you can buy other aircraft of the same type with no negotiation at all. The folks advertising their planes for sale will gladly sell their plane at their **FULL** advertised priced. Can you blame them in this market? They are your seller's competition.

Before you make an offer you should give your seller an opportunity to express his pricing aspiration.

What is he asking for his airplane?

Would he accept the median selling price?

As far as you know, he had not thought of selling before he got your letter. His willingness to meet up at the "first look" inspection point is proof positive that he has considered your interest and is ready to move forward. He may not have previously been thinking about selling but he is now and that's all that matters. It is safe to imagine that he has at least done some thinking about what he'd like to get for his airplane.

You could simply ask him what he'd take for his airplane.

DON'T!!!!!!

The straight forward method can quickly descend into angry words, hurt feelings and no sale. A better strategy is to work through the numbers together. Attempt it only after you have decided at what number you'd being willing to buy and at what number you'd rather take a pass.

Would you pay more than the median asking price for his plane?

Why?

How much higher would you be willing to go?

Once you know your range, call the seller.

Start by thanking him for coming to the inspection airport and for sending along his **Pilot's Log Book**.

Next, tell him that you would like to own his airplane. Explain that you are ready to discuss price and that once you agree on a price you will escrow the agreed amount to be released pending a clean title search and an **annual** inspection to be performed at your airport by your IA.

Make double certain he understands that you will pay for the annual, his travel expenses, the title search and the escrow fees. If he agrees you will setup escrow with one of the aviation escrow companies located in Oklahoma City.

Here are a few names you may consider:

AIC Title Service LLC
Powell Aircraft Title Service
King Aircraft Title, Inc.
Insured Aircraft Title Service

Before he can answer, ask him this obligating question. **"Are you ready to part with your airplane?"** Doubtless he will answer that he is.

The terms of the offer include more than price. Verify that he's willing to fly the plane to your home airport for the annual. Reiterate that you'll stand for all of the expenses including his return trip. Be firm on this request.

Typically he'll want to know why you are running an annual rather than a pre-buy which would be cheaper. Your response is simple, "the pre-buy is dead money and the annual gives me a year's flying before I have to do it again. I get something for my money."

If this airplane is IFR equipped and will be used for that purpose you will want to have the transponder and pitot/static system check and certification performed at the same time. Have all of the avionics checked. You will be paying for this as well so there is no reason for the owner to object.

Quickly tell him that you aren't certain what a fair price for the aircraft should be. Accordingly, you have done some research and uncovered the current median asking price for airplanes like his and then quickly give him that number. If he doesn't say anything, quickly mention that you have no way of knowing what the actual median selling price is and there is no way to uncover it.

Mention that with sales being as slow as they are for as long as they have been that the median selling price is likely to be much lower than the median asking price. If he is still breathing and isn't yet screaming; it's time to suggest a price.

"I am prepared to escrow the funds today and close the deal as early as next week. Twenty percent under the median asking price looks fair to me. Is it acceptable to you? " There may well be some back and forth. Just remember your boundaries and don't go above them.

Be sure to put your understanding of your mutual agreement in writing. Honest misunderstandings happen. Party A doesn't hear what Party B said the same way that Party B intended. A written document spells everything out so everyone has a complete understanding of the deal going in.

The written document must stipulate the aircraft to be purchased and its current equipment list. It should use the aircraft's common name (*Cessna 150 for example*) as well as its serial number and "N" number. The current number of hours on the aircraft, engine and prop at the time of the offer should be stated. The airplanes current condition should be stated including known issues and discrepancies. **It must be recorded that other than these stipulated issues the airplane has NO known squawks and if any are discovered prior to the completion of this sale the present owner will at his expense have them repaired or replaced to the Buyer's satisfaction.**

All liens and encumbrances must be spelled out and the current owner acknowledges that they will be satisfied prior to final payment. A through title search will be accomplished at the **BUYER's** expense. A purchase price is spelled out and that amount is escrowed with an agreed upon escrow company.

An annual inspection of the airframe, engine and propeller will be accomplished at a time and place designated by the buyer. The costs of the inspection will be borne by the buyer. A transponder and pitot/static system check and certification will be accomplished at the same time and place as well as a check of the complete avionics system all at the buyer's expense.

The buyer agrees to pay the sellers reasonable and appropriate travel cost for bringing the aircraft to the buyers designated inspection point and for his travel back to his home. Once the inspection is completed and all squawks are satisfactorily dealt with the buyer agrees to release the escrowed purchase funds to the seller and the seller agrees to release full clear title to the buyer.

It isn't really a hard document to prepare. Before you spend one nickel with an attorney make certain that you and the seller agree to a draft which you and he construct. This agreement merely reduces to writing all of the points that you have already agreed too verbally.

Here are four simple rules that should carry you safely through the negotiating process:

- **Know the numbers before you begin negotiating.**
- **Be ready to walk away from a deal you don't like.**
- **Make a low but reasonable offer and sweeten the deal by raising it in small increments as necessary.**
- **Put it in writing and get it signed**

Chapter VII

The Final Exam

The BIG Idea: Trust but Verify.

What if the seller agrees to have the annual done but insists that his IA do it at his airport. Your response is easy. You agree to the suggestion but counter that your IA **MUST** be present and that the buyer **MUST** pay for the annual. If it comes to your IA you pay, if it goes to his IA he pays. If the seller refuses to have an annual done by anyone but will accept a "pre-buy" inspection, you decline and move on to the next aircraft. Having the plane annualed before the purchase goes through is a very important negotiating point.

Here's why.

A discovery made during a "pre-buy" inspection is not binding and the "pre-buy" inspection results are not recorded in the aircraft, engine and propeller log books. If something is uncovered in a "pre-buy" inspection and the owner decides to do nothing about it, he merely fires up his engine and flies back home.

Things are a little different with an annual inspection. The annual and its findings will be recorded in the log books. If the compressions are low, their actual readings will be entered. If they are below sixty the IA can find that the aircraft is not airworthy. If they are below seventy but above sixty, the buyer can ask the owner to TOP the engine.

Other things will come up during the annual and the owner **MUST** deal with all of them. Some could ground the airplane until repaired and some can be put off until he gets home but his log book will show the issue. An annual dramatically increases the buyer's leverage and greatly intensifies the seller's desire to complete the sale.

Prior to the annual the seller has stipulated that the aircraft is free of squawks other than those he has listed and presented to the buyer. The buyer has agreed to accept the aircraft and complete the sale with those squawks and only those squawks.

Annuals often turn up problems; big ones and little ones; expensive ones and cheap ones. The IA will quantify each of them by providing a squawk list and his estimate to do the repairs. He will also let it be known which of the squawks affect the planes airworthiness. Obviously the cost of these repairs can impact the offer you previously made for the aircraft. If the repairs do not affect airworthiness they do not need to be made for the annual to be entered in the log book and the aircraft returned to service. Either you or the seller can then legally fly the airplane exactly as it is.

If you still want to buy, make a "final offer" by saying, "These repairs have to be made before I will close on this airplane. The moment they are completed I am prepared to close at the agreed price. You can have the repairs made here or someplace else. That's up to you. If you take it someplace else the cost of delivery back to me will be on you. Further, you must pay for the annual; I will gladly reimburse you when the sale is completed."

That's a mouthful. Let's unpack it a bit. You just said that you want to buy the airplane at the price previously agreed upon. You are not asking for a price reduction and you won't accept a price increase. The matter of the repairs is a separate item and they are **HIS** problem not yours. You will complete the purchase only when the plane is squawk free. The buyer has been informed that your IA who did the inspection is willing to do the repairs or the buyer can take the airplane someplace else. In either event you will pay for his travel expenses to the annual as previously agreed and of course for the cost of the annual **once the repairs have been made**. If he moves the airplane someplace else for the repairs you have no way of knowing that the repairs will actually be made and that the sale will finalize. He may instead fly home and chalk-up the experience to a bad life lesson leaving you with the costs of his travel and the annual and have no airplane to show for your trouble.

Basically, the discovery of the non-disclosed squawks terminated the original deal. You are no longer obligated to pay for the annual and his travel expenses under the terms of the initial deal and you do not have to complete the purchase as the seller has misrepresented the condition of his aircraft. He is obligated to bring it up to the specs he represented to you or the deal is off.

The new offer you are now making requires him to have your IA do the repairs at the seller's expense. When he says no that the repairs will only be done by his IA at his airport he is throwing a "fly into the ointment". Your suggestion that he front the cost of the annual and his travel expenses is merely insurance that he will actually have the repairs done and finalize the sale. It is important that you tell the seller your reasons. He can certainly refuse but it forces him to "lay his cards on the table".

The seller will be unhappy. He is being asked to spend money on an airplane he will no longer own and he will doubtless disagree with some of the issues *"your"* IA has identified and his estimated repair costs. Your big job now is to get him re-committed to the deal. If not, you have both wasted time and money. That's not a good outcome for you or the seller. It is a "lose-lose".

Explain carefully that there is an alternative. If he merely reduces the price of the airplane by an amount equal to the costs of the estimated repairs he will go home with cash and you will deal with the repairs. The risk of further issues being discovered as the repairs are made is yours not his as you will be the aircraft's owner not him.

Listen carefully to what he has to say next; the words he is using and the way he is using them. Is he prepared to be reasonable or is just angry?

Suggest that he give his IA a call and go through the squawks and repair estimates with him. That typically takes a lot of the sting out of the problem. What happens next will depend on how motivated he is to sell and how angry he is. If he'd like to be rid of this airplane and fill his bank account with your money then it will end well. If not, you have a decision to make. You are still in control. You could still buy his airplane at the agreed price and pay for the repairs yourself or you can play brinksmanship and stand to lose the airplane.

Let's say that he appears intractable and that he is ready to not go through with the deal. Explain the situation to him in a way he hasn't yet considered.

Say something like this, "I understand how you feel. Clearly you didn't expect any new issues to be found with your airplane and you obviously don't want to pay to have them repaired as it reduces the net you'll realize on this sale. I understand that. Please appreciate that I didn't expect there to be any issues with your airplane either. If I pay to have them repaired then I am paying more for the airplane than you agreed to sell it to me for and I don't think I am willing to do that at this point. If you want to back out of this deal, I totally understand. Consider this though, you are going to have to pay the cost of the annual and you are going to have to pay for your own travel costs here and back. My offer to pay for those items was contingent on buying the airplane at the price I offered with no squawks other than the ones you stipulated. You'll leave with a fresh annual and nothing else. My strong preference is that we stay on track. You should pay for the repairs and I'll pay for the annual, your travel costs and release the escrowed funds for the airplane."

Once faced with the reality of having to pay for the annual and the travel costs, I have never had a seller refuse to pay for the repairs and rush to complete the sale. In all cases they have simply agreed to lower the cost of the airplane by the cost of the repairs. The question always comes up about splitting the cost of the repairs. I always decline and explain that I'm not asking them to split the travel and annual costs.

The final offer is always the escrowed offer. **I pay exactly what I promised to pay and they provide a squawk free machine just as they said they would.** No one I have ever bought a plane from has gone away mad or felt they have been treated unfairly. Everyone I have bought an airplane from becomes a friend.

Treat people fairly and demand the same in return. That's the way to do "win-win" business.

My Favorites

What follows are a few pictures of the airplane types I have personally owned and flown. Each is special. I liked them all. Every pilot has a favorites list, this one is mine. I hope you enjoy looking at it. Let me be clear, most of these pictures are of sisterships rather than the actually machine I touched.

A fresh pile of Damage History!

(These airplanes were rolled into a common ball by a hurricane spawned tornado that marched across the Daytona Beach Airport. These machines were all part of the Embry-Riddle fleet.)

Low & Slow

(Not every airplane you'll own was built for cross country travel. Here's a great example.)

Aeronca 65 TCA

(There were 8 civilian aircraft in the air over Oahu at time of the December 7th Japanese sneak attack on Pearl Harbor. One was an Aeronca 65 TCA)

My personal favorite low and slow machine.

(The Ercoupe 415C has been a wonderful certified airplane since the early 1940's. Today it is also classified as an LSA. No medical required.)

Landing a taildragger requires skill.

(The Piper Pacer was replaced by Piper Tripacer. The ease of landing with its successor's tricycle gear quickly chased the Pacer from the Piper manufacturing line.)

Light twins are still the speed merchants of the GA Fleet

(The Baron's impressive cruise is matched by modern straight-legged, single engine airplanes.)

Diamond DA-42 Twinstar

(This diesel powered twin failed to match its pre-delivery hype. It failed to meet any of its major design goals and became a major disappointment for all involved.)

Game Changer

(Cirrus' groundbreaking SR series took the market by storm from the first production shipments in 1999 until today. More new Cirrus' are shipped today than any other single engine aircraft.)

The Lancair 400

(It is touted as the world's fastest single engine production aircraft easily beating many light twins as well. Cessna bought Lancair and found a way to grab defeat from the jaws of victory.)

Piper Cherokee 140

(Faced with the success of the Cessna 172, Piper replaced the tube and fabric Tripacer with the more modern all aluminum Cherokee. Most Piper aircraft since have been based on this airframe. I owned the one pictured above. It was the vehicle for my instrument training.)

Cessna 172 Skyhawk

(The Skyhawk is the most successful, manufactured light aircraft in history. Nothing else comes close to matching its sales. Two doors, four seats, 115 knot cruise, relatively low fuel burn, what's not to like?)

Cessna 182 Skylane

(Since its birth in 1957, the Cessna 182 has been one of the most popular planes in the sky. It has decent cruise speed and range PLUS it is said to be able to carry anything you can squeeze into its cabin and still manage to close the doors.)

Cessna 206 Stationair

(The sport-utility vehicle of the air pretty much sums up this wonderful offering from Cessna. The fuel burn is hard on your pocket but if you can stand the pain at the pump this is really worth looking at, particularly the turbo version. In a word – NICE.)

Nothing gets more performance from each horsepower than a Mooney.

(The Mooney M20A pictured above is famous for its wooden wing.)

Piper T-Tailed Lance

(Reasonable speed, reasonable range, reasonable payload, the
Lance is a good cross country choice. It represents a great
value as many buyers don't like the t-tail, the average asking
price will reflect what I call a "desirability" discount.)

EuroFox

(The EuroFox is one of the many LSA's that have hit the market. Few used LSA's are available due to the newness of the category.)

SELL HIGH

Chapter VIII

Timing is everything!

The BIG Idea: Sell ONLY when the market is hot.

Buy in the winter!

Sell in the summer!

In the summer pilots' fancies turn to airplanes. We'll pay any price for something that flies. Patience goes out the window. Getting into the air **NOW** becomes the name of the game.

In the dark, cold days of winter most pilots are ground bound by really unpleasant weather. Their hangar and insurance bills pile up like driven snow. A depressed owner is often pleased to find a buyer, any buyer and he'll settle for a really low price. Patience goes out the window. Getting rid of it **NOW** is the name of the game.

If it's the middle of November when the sell bug bites you, **WAIT!**

"Fools rush in where angels fear to tread."

Relax, breathe deep and take your time. Oddly enough patience is more important when you're selling than when you're buying.

The BIG 5 rules for selling are:

1. Know why you're selling
2. Know what you will be **BUYING**.
3. Get your airplane ready to sell
4. Know what your machine is worth
5. Sell **ONLY** when the market is hot

Rule number one in the aircraft selling business is to know exactly **WHY** you want to sell your present aircraft. Potential buyers are gonna' ask and they won't buy unless they get a really good answer.

I knew a man who ran an ad to sell his plane that began ***"Poor health forces sale."***

That's a good headline for an ad. As far as I knew, this fellow had never been sick a day in his life. I asked him about the ad. He said, "The ad is correct, my poor health is forcing the sale. I hate that fugitive from the maintenance hangar. Just getting near it makes me sick!"

That was his reason, what's yours?

A pilot I know lusted for a Bellanca Super Viking, which is a very nice airplane offering impressive cross country performance. His lust eventually turned into an obsession as the thing invaded his dreams. Soon he had bags under his eyes from lack of sleep. Every sentence he spoke began with "Bellanca Super Viking this" or "Bellanca Super Viking that". He was hooked.

Quickly he traded his nearly perfect straight tail Cessna 182 to move on up. He had never flown in, let alone piloted a Bellanca Super Viking before making his fateful decision. ***"Gotta-Have-It-Itis"*** had him so completely that he did the deal over the phone, sight unseen.

The dealer provided two hours of transition training. Big Ed is a masterful pilot and caught on quickly. The problem was shoe horning him into the pilot's chair. Unlike his Cessna, the Bellanca has only one door and it's on the right side of the aircraft.

Big Ed literally had to roll across the cockpit to reach the pilot's seat. That performance, while worth the price of admission to watch, was preceded by an unceremonious crawl up the low wing to reach the cabin door.

Big Ed is a gazelle as a pilot but a fish out of water when ground bound. Graceful will never be his middle name.

Bellancas are roomier than Mooneys but cramped compared to Cessnas particularly 182 Cessnas. Big Ed loved the way the airplane flew but putting it on finally proved too much for him.

Over time he flew less and less. Eventually, the Super Viking became a lonely "hangar queen". Its last two annuals have shown zero hours of use for the entire year.

Knowing where you are going is equally good advice for navigation or aircraft buying. Would Big Ed have traded his Cessna 182 for a Bellanca Super Viking if he had spent some time flying one? The needle of the Truth Meter is stuck on **NO.**

Big Ed's mistake wasn't picking the wrong airplane. In fact, he picked a great airplane. It is a great airplane for someone else's missions not his. He got caught up in the fantasy of flying at high altitude and high speed to faraway places. That was his mistake, don't let it be yours.

The Bellanca Super Viking is a terrific choice, if you have a cross country need. Big Ed is retired. Local flights of less than one hour's duration are 100% of his mission. He did not need and could not take advantage of the benefits of his new high flying, go fast machine and suffered mightily at the hand of its shortcomings.

If he had just slowed down and dealt with why the 182 wasn't making him smile anymore he could have saved a lot of time, a ton of money and still been an active pilot. Instead, he has become a disappointed has-been-aviator who has a giant paper weight in his once happy hangar.

When the lust bug bites you, and it will, consider the use of the airplane of your dreams before you reach for your wallet but first figure out why you are tired of your current ride.

An airplane is a mission rated machine. There is no one size fits all airplane. Has your mission really changed? Why does your current airplane no longer satisfy you?

Big Ed's mission hadn't changed a lick and if he truly thought it had he could have used his 182 for many, many cross country adventures as a "show me" experiment. If he had just tried out that side of flying before committing to it he would have kept the 182.

A single mission definition can't be assigned to my flying needs. I'll bet the same is true for you.

Most times I am best served by a low and slow Burger Hunter. Often I need *(really need)* a go fast, cross country machine, the faster it flies the better. When I was working on my commercial rating a complex airplane was required.

Last year my heart turned to an amphibian as I read Richard Bach's wonderful book about *Puff* his SeaRey. I dreamt of spending time bone fishing in the Bahamas in a cove seldom visited by anyone but me and my SeaRey or maybe my Lake or perhaps a my new Flight Design on floats or better yet an old Cub on floats.

I fantasize about planes and the places they can take me a lot. We pilots are all like that.

The planes that have lived in my hangar and yours are tributes to compromise. They must wear many hats. The job of a thoughtful owner is to prioritize needs. A two place airplane won't work for family trips or most business trips. What about those low and slow moments?

You can slow a Bonanza down by pulling the throttle back but you can never whip a 172 hard enough to catch a Bonanza. So which do you do most; cross country jaunts or fall foliage flights and weekend burger runs?

Analysis works for the head but it is unsatisfying for the heart. The heart wants what the heart wants.

Your first step when being over taken by new airplane lust is to embrace it. Immediately re-read Chapter's one and two of this book and add in a **NEW** step.

Call everyone within three hundred miles of your home 'port who has a set of your must have wings advertised for sale. Arrange to see and fly as many as you can by finding sellers that are willing to demo their ship if you buy the fuel. Explain that you are early in your hunt for a plane of this type. Leading people on creates bad karma after all. The truth always works, BS seldom does.

Your purpose is to get a feel for what is available that can be seen and touched not merely dreamt about. Since we are dealing primarily with used airplanes not new ones our purchasing decision is limited to what's available. Sometimes the entire available fleet has been *"rode hard and put up wet"*.

Nothing will chase lust from a young man's heart quicker than seeing his dream girl without her makeup on or his dream airplane up close and personal rather than in a stream of Photoshopped pictures.

It is important to fly over in your current machine. The comparison will be unavoidable and unembellished. Let's say you're dreaming of a Bonanza and will be moving up from a Cessna 182.

Reality check number one comes when you crawl over the co-pilot seat to get into the Bo's captain chair. It doesn't have a cockpit door on the left side only the right and you have to do some wing walking to get there. For a Cessna guy that's an issue.

For a Cessna guy's wife it can be a deal killer. Its supper tough to wing walk in five inch heels. Take 'em off for boarding and learn just how quickly the "no slip" material covering the walkway can shred a pair of nylons. Cessna wives do not cotton to Bonanza wing walking.

That's the first splash of cold water on this dream ship but it won't likely be the last. What if it just doesn't suit your needs?

Simple!

Find what type does and don't dump your current bird until you do. Having something to fly is better than having nothing to fly. Having something to fly helps you ward off the rush to marry up with the first type of plane that *'might'* work. You're looking for a marriage after all not a one night stand.

Let's say that all goes well. The type of plane you've been dreaming about actually works for you and after due consideration it fits your new mission in a way that your current bird just can't.

Remember this, though, above all else - **Sell before you buy.** Once you are certain that a particular type meets your needs and your finances allow you to have one that is.

When you know what you want make a plan to go and get it. Don't wind up with more airplanes than you need and please don't worry that the world will run out of the type airplane you want or that the only perfect example is the one you just flew.

The airplane you should buy will be available when you're ready to buy. That's a fact.

If its fall or winter, use the time to get your machine ready for the market. Sell in the summer! A&Ps are underworked in the winter and over worked in the summer. Make an honest squawk list and have everything fixed! Everything!!!!!!

Please sit down and get you logbooks into nice readable order. Then scan every page of every document the seller should see and create a file that's ready to transmit.

Then deal with your ships appearance. Tears in the upholstery, cracks in the plastic, scratched paint and crazed windows all need to be repaired or replaced. Have your machine washed, waxed and detailed so it looks like your "pride and joy". No buyer will believe that it's better than it looks. Getting all of this work done will take much longer than you imagine.

Find a professional photographer experienced with aircraft *(don't do it yourself)* and have him take pictures of your machine; the good, the bad and the ugly. Make certain that the date isn't stamped on the front of each photo. Then do a video walk around as well as an action video or two.

What about price?

Step one in setting the price is to forget about how much money you'll need to buy the next plane. Force any thoughts of the next plane out of your mind. For now, you're a seller not a buyer. Remember that!!!

Research the market. What's for sale and what is the median price of what's *for sale*? Forget that your plane is better *(it probably isn't)*.

List your plane at 20% *UNDER* the market.

The **BEST** day to start your sales campaign is May 1st. Winter is way over, spring has sprung and summer hasn't blossomed.

Oddly enough, there will be fewer planes offered for sale in the summer as their owners are too busy enjoying them to consider parting with them. Summer brings more buyers and fewer sellers.

This combination can't help but drive the price meter up. Take advantage of it!

Chapter IX

What's the Deal?

The BIG Idea: Never wing it when offering your airplane for sale?

Many people consider only **PRICE** when preparing to sell their airplane. That's an error equal to bringing a knife to a gun fight.

Are you sure you have clear title?

Who will pay for the inspection, transfer and delivery costs?

How will payment be made?

Will you take a trade?

Will you finance the purchase?

How long are you on the hooks to take the plane back after it has been sold? "Used" airplanes are covered by the "lemon laws" of many states.

Let's first explore the thing called price.

As an aircraft seller you will be doing everything differently than you did as an aircraft buyer. Boundaries are good things for countries and aircraft sellers. Set them early. Know what you are prepared to accept before you list your machine for sale and how exactly you are prepared to accept it. For most sellers, the asking price is merely a starting place. We all know that used car salesman's game. Don't play it. Be refreshingly different.

Don't start high and later settle low.

To sell it quickly, price it low!

Don't worry about "leaving money on the table" you won't.

Actually, a high price is the best way I know to insure that you "leave money on the table".

A high price attracts fewer prospects.

On the other hand, everyone who is seriously looking for a plane of your type will pick-up the phone and throw their hat into the ring for a great plane offered at a low price. Someone will pay exactly what you are asking and do so on your terms.

To set the perfect price, calculate the average asking price for all planes of your type currently advertised for sale. Forget what you paid for it. Forget all of the money you spent to bring it up to specs. Forget everything except its **current market value**.

Could you comfortably accept 20% lower than the market average? Forget what you'd like to have and concentrate only on what you **MUST** have.

At 20% under the market's current asking price your machine will move while others sit. Yours will be the "go to" ad. Everyone who is seriously interested in buying a plane like yours will call you!

That's a fact.

Two caveats.

First, your airplane has to at least equal the average airplane in every respect. Second, you have to be ready to move it **NOW!** The phone will ring; serious buyers will be **HIGHLY** motivated and ready to act. They will not want to risk losing out on your offer.

Be certain this price satisfies your financial requirements. If not don't bother.

Issue number one in aircraft selling is proof of ownership. Do you have clear title to your airplane? You may think you do and you may be very wrong. Call the escrow company that you plan to use for the transaction and have them run a title search. You'll rest easy and you can document clear title to any potential buyer. If there are problems, now is the time to get them taken care of.

There is still much to do before placing your ad. Start with the log books. You **MUST** have them all since the airplane left the factory and they must be complete. Not having the logs drops the value of your airplane by one third. Never buy a plane without great logs and you'll avoid this problem when it's time to sell.

By **ALL** of the logs I mean, the engine log, the airframe log, the propeller log and your pilot's log. These log books are the bare minimum proofs of a well-cared for airplane. The first three show how the airplane was maintained the later one shows how the airplane was flown and by whom.

Next, make certain that your AD and SB logs are up-to-date and that **ALL** AD's and SB's are accounted for and current. Every receipt that you have for the airplane should be kept in a three ring binder.

Once you have assembled and organized this material, scan it into a PDF file. The moment a prospect sends in his earnest money deposit you can send these files to him if he requests them but not before. The earnest money deposit is his key to your information trove. If the prospect isn't ready to commit he hasn't earned the right to see your logs. Simple as that.

Your paper work should be fairly easy to prepare. Keeping these items up-to-date and filed properly should be a matter of course for any conscientious owner.

Getting the ship ready is a judgment call. Is there any issue that you feel should be taken care of before you sell? Talk to your IA; is he aware of anything on your aircraft that should be taken care of even if it doesn't affect airworthiness?

Schedule an annual inspection as well as the pitot-static and transponder re-certification for mid-April. Make it clear that you need the airplane in your hangar by the last week of April.

Have the plane washed, waxed and detailed when it leaves the maintenance hangar. You want it looking amazing for the photo shoot.

Hire a first rate photographer with aviation experience. Have him take a ream of photos. Make certain to document ALL plus and minus areas. If there are hangar rash dings make certain they are documented. If the carpets are brand new make certain the photos show how great they look.

Finally, do a video of the airplane describing all of its plus features using the **Sell the Sizzle** techniques we'll discuss in a later chapter and take a few action video of it in flight. Do not post photos or videos with your aircraft for sale ad. Their purpose is to close interested prospects not to fire the imagination of "Lookie Lou's".

When the plane is ready there is still plenty of work to be done before placing your ad.

What are the terms of payment that you will accept? Interest rates have never been lower and that's a good thing but the banks have never been stingier and that's a bad thing. Credit worthy pilots can't get loans to become aircraft owners. The same is true for would be home purchasers. Our economy is healing but it isn't yet running on all cylinders.

Will you finance this sale? If the answer is yes the term "owner financing available" placed in your ad will bring forth twice as many prospects. That's the good news.

No credit sale is as safe as a cash sale. That's for sure. There are a few steps you can take to protect yourself.

First let's talk price. The cash price and the owner financed price are not necessarily the same. If you are going to take the risk you have to be paid to do so. A good rule of thumb is to offer owner financing at the market's current average asking price which is 20% higher than your cash price.

Set the interest rate at 5% which is higher than current home mortgage rates, lower than typical automobile finance rate and a bargain when compared to credit card interest rates.

The down payment should be no less than 30% and the term no more than five years. You are trying to help a purchaser achieve the dream of aircraft ownership but you aren't trying to "take him to raise".

The other terms of an owner financed purchase are certainly firm but not unfair. The finance contract you will establish with the purchaser is a "contract for deed" type. Simply put, the title remains 100% yours until the buyer makes his final payment. It's hard enough to repossess an airplane from a "dead beat" buyer without having to jump through hoops to reclaim the title. If the buyer stops making his payments you can with proper notice repossess the aircraft legally and sell it to someone else that same afternoon.

The contract for owner financing must also specify the additional duties of the buyer. Keeping the airplane in good condition is an absolute requirement. He must agree to have the oil changed every twenty-five hours, have an oil analysis run and to email you necessary documentation to prove that he is complying.

Once a year he must fly the airplane back to your airport for its annual inspection which will be accomplished by your IA at the buyers expense. If it can be shown that the aircraft is not being maintained properly then the contract must state that you have the right to repossess it following notice being given and a reasonable cure period assigned.

The airplane must be hangared not tied down and you must be given a key to the hangar and the right to make unannounced visits for the purpose of inspecting the plane.

Obviously, setting up an owner financed purchase requires the services of a very skilled attorney. **DO NOT** attempt drafting this agreement on your own.

Here's the list of the remaining issues you **MUST** settle before your plane goes on the market. I call it the **Dirty Dozen plus Three**:

1. Who's the Escrow agent?
2. How long from opening of Escrow to closing the sale?
3. Is the sale *"as is"*?
4. Will a pre-purchase inspection occur?
5. Where and by whom?
6. Who pays for the inspection?
7. Who pays for travel to and from the inspection?
8. If repairs are required, who pays?
9. Is the sale *"where is"*?
10. Who delivers the airplane?
11. Who pays the delivery expenses?
12. What is the purchase price?
13. What are the payment terms?
14. Who pays sales tax?
15. Will your attorney formalize our agreement?

Chapter X

Sell the Sizzle not the Steak!

The BIG Idea: The quickest route to a buyer's wallet goes through his heart not his head.

In 1974 William Morrow published **Zen and the Art of Motorcycle Maintenance: An Inquiry into Values** by Robert Pirsig. In it Mr. Pirsig's main character Phaedrus points out that *"it isn't what a thing is but what a thing does that's important."*

I have quoted Phaedrus during every sales seminar I have ever given. It is the essence of the consultive selling process. Forget about all of the technical aspects of the airplane you own and the specifications of its engine and avionics. The buyer knows all of that already.

Selling the Sizzle not the Steak is all about **WHY** and has little to do with not **WHAT**.

You don't order a steak because it's a fine source of protein.

You order it because it smells good and makes your mouth water. It sounds hot and juicy when it sizzles on the plate every high-end steakhouse sets before you. You don't need that big plate lapping steak but you most certainly want it. Satisfying **WANTS** not **NEEDS** is what makes sales happen.

Restaurants **NEVER** talk about their product specs. Their TV commercials draw you in with wonderful pictures of perfectly prepared food. They practice **WANT** generation selling. The reason is simple. People make emotional decisions quickly. Intellectual decisions take a long time. Restaurants rely on impulse buying.

Advertising an airplane for sale is about making the phone ring. No one will buy an airplane from an ad. What should be in a good ad that accomplishes that objective?

VERY LITTLE.

The less said the better.

If you state the year and model of your airplane and list all of its avionics, the engine time, the airframe time and attach photos of the exterior, the interior and the panel you will have an ad that is average. You should expect average results, meaning few if any phone calls.

Why would anybody call? You told them everything they needed to know to **disqualify** your airplane from their short list in the ad.

It has too many hours on the engine or maybe not enough. It doesn't have the panel they really want. It has the wrong autopilot. They hate the color or don't like the paint scheme.

That's how we discriminate when buying anything. We first screen out then we screen in. The problem with an ad is that it gives the seller no way to handle a prospect's objections. No way at all. The first bad impression of the potential buyer goes unchallenged. That's a really bad idea.

Consider this when writing your ad. Nothing in it can be objectionable to anyone. No way can argue with an engine time if they don't know it. Remember all that you're trying to do is make the phone ring so **YOU** can sell the plane. The ad needs only to state the type airplane, the year model, your phone number, your email address, the price you're asking and a few superlatives.

Why would anyone call on such a low information ad with no pictures? What would make them want to learn more about this plane?

That's where price and superlative statements come into play.

First let's study superlatives. These sizzle statements can be universal like, **"World's Best Cessna 150"** or **"Perfect Cessna 150"**, **"The Perfect 10 of Cessna 150's"** or **"Professional Pilot's Pampered Cessna 150"** or **"Amazing 1974 Cessna 150"**.

Specific superlatives target individual features and exclude all others. **"Lowest Time Cessna 150 in America!"** or **"Complete IFR Panel!"**

Superlatives are interest builders but they won't make your prospect reach for his phone and start mashing numbers. That's the job of a **LOW** asking price but only when it is preceded by a superlative statement. A low asking price will scare customers away unless they have reason to believe that this plane represents great value. First they have to want the plane then they have to be called to action by the price.

A superlative lead-in followed by a low price tells everyone that this plane will sell quickly. You don't have to say it and you shouldn't. Statements like **"Won't last long!"** come straight off of a used car lot. Don't use them.

Here's an ad that will make the phone ring for a Cessna 150. Let's assume that the average asking price is $22,000.

World's Best 1974 Cessna 150
Value priced at $17,500
(555) 345-1212
me@myemail.com

For a moment, place yourself into a mythical prospect's mind. If you are seriously interested in buying a 1974 Cessna 150 why would you not make an inquiry on this one?

What, if anything, screens it out?

What, if anything, drops it off of your *"to be considered"* **list.**

The answer to both questions is nothing.

Your email will ping and your phone will ring. No one seriously looking for a late model Cessna 150 will be able to resist responding to this ad. That is, no one who is interested in a late model Cessna 150 who actually **SEES** this ad will be able to resist it.

Key to **Selling the Sizzle and Not the Steak** is to get the word out everywhere and to do so all at once.

Here's how.

A word ad containing no pictures is **CHEAP** to run. That's a good thing. You won't have to wonder if you should advertise in **Trade-A-Plane** or **The Controller** or both or either. You place the ad with every website and every print publication that takes advertisements for planes for sale like yours.

Appendix C is the list I use. To it you **MUST** add, the aircraft type club's print and/or web based newsletter. Don't stop there, do as much research as you can and find as many places to advertise as you can. I always drop one in my local newspaper.

Two more advertising paths should be followed.

First, make a one page sales brochure for your machine and send multiple copies to all of the FBO's and flight schools at all of the airports within 300 miles of your home airport. A very high percentage of all the used airplanes sold each year find their new home with 300 miles of their old home. That's a fact.

Make certain that every pilot you have ever met gets a copy of the brochure. Make certain that everyone at your local airport knows that your airplane is actively for sale. Slip it under every hangar door at your home airport just to make sure.

The phone will ring.

When it does, take control of the call. Ask very quickly about the prospect's aviation background and why he is shopping for a plane like yours.

Before he has a chance to ask about your plane, ask him what he is looking for in his new plane and what items are most important to him. In other words, ask him to tell you how to sell him. Don't simply answer his questions about your airplane.

In the chapter titled, **"What's the Deal"** we discussed how important it is to have your plane in tip-top condition before bringing it to market.

Here's where **Sizzle Selling** comes into its own.

Start at the pointy end. Mention that your airplane has a **Buy with Confidence** engine. With only 650 hours in the log book it is **below mid-time**. The cylinder compressions were taken at the aircraft's annual just last week. They are all in **out of the box condition** with each reading in the mid to high seventies. The most recent oil analysis report was also taken last week and it showed **a good as new** engine with no unusual substances or metal in the oil which matched all previous reports. The engine logs are complete demonstrating this to be **a pride of ownership** machine ever since the engine and airplane left the factory. It has been overhauled just once and that was five years ago. Total time on the **gently used** engine is under 3,000 hours. The IA boroscoped and recorded each cylinder during last week's annual. They are in **factory fresh condition** showing no rust and no pitting.

Buy with confidence, below mid-time, out of the box condition, good as new, pride of ownership, gently used and **factory fresh,** are all **Sizzle Selling** superlative terms.

How could any serious prospect dismiss purchasing this aircraft on the basis of the engine? You haven't just said that the engine is trouble free you've proved it eight ways from Sunday with more supporting data than any buyer could hope for. He doesn't have to take your word for any of it which is why you began your pitch with the engine. Money pit number one for any airplane owner is the engine.

Let's pretend that he has told you that he just completed his PPL and has decided to pursue an IFR endorsement for his new ticket. That is a perfect opening for you to pitch the panel.

In the "**What's the Deal**" chapter we encouraged you to get the pitot static system and the transponder checks done with the annual. If you did, you can now say these words.

"You'll be glad to know that this airplane was **re-certified for two more years of instrument flight** just last week. It has an **instructor preferred** panel setup with two digital nav/coms, two VOR indicators, a glide slope indicator, a push button audio panel with three light marker beacon indicator lights and an approach certified GPS. You'll **train with confidence** knowing that you can **pass the IFR practical examination** with this panel and **transition easily** to the high-performance, cross country airplane you will one day own.

Never spew a list of product numbers and specs and hope that he interprets their meaning correctly and is impressed with your aircraft's equipment list. What's important is to let him know how the boxes in your panel will get him to his goal and beyond.

The **Sizzle Selling** terms used to present the panel target his stated training requirement, **re-certified for two more years of**

instrument flying, instructor preferred, train with confidence, pass the IFR practical examination and **transition easily.**

Here's what you communicated without arguing the details and layout of your panel. The panel is good to go for the next two years, taking no money out of his pocket while he chases his instrument rating. Any instructor he decides to work with will be pleased with this panel as everything he needs to learn and master instrument flying is present. He can train with confidence knowing that the panel he is training behind will be suitable for his practical exam. Last but not least, that approach certified GPS will allow him to transition to his next airplane without missing a beat. He'll know GPS approaches like the back of his hand. The GPS in his next machine will probably change but not its use.

The method and the message are simple. Help your prospect by understanding what his needs are and showing him precisely how your airplane satisfies them. He doesn't need a factory new engine. What he needs is a reliable engine that isn't going to break his piggy bank with constant stays in the maintenance hangar. The same is true for the panel. Find out what he intends to do with the airplane and then show him how your panel satisfies his requirements.

You can control the sale using this "**consultative approach**" to "**needs satisfaction selling.**"

That's what wins.

What loses is "**specification selling**".

You either match every spec. the prospects has in mind, which is practically impossible, or you try to argue him into believing that your specification is better than his. In other words you have to get him to admit that he is wrong and you are right. Good luck with that!

Assuming you are successful, what makes your plane better than the other fifty (50) he is looking at? You have no chance to convince him that you are a better buy **qualitatively** since this has descended into a spec matching exercise. Hence all that you can do is to compete **quantitatively**, meaning you have to match all of the specs and have the lowest price.

Selling the Sizzle not the Steak is all about matching needs not specs.

Chapter XI

Turning Interest into Offers

The BIG Idea: It's time to count the cash and turn over the keys.

Everything you did as a buyer you don't do as a seller. That's rule number one.

Your plane never leaves your airfield. If the buyer wants a complete copy of the logs and he should, you email them **AFTER** he puts up a deposit.

If the buyer wants to see the airplane and he should, have him come to your field.

If the buyer wants to fly the airplane and he should, he sits in the right seat, you sit in the left and he buys the fuel.

If the buyer wants a pre-buy inspection, have him bring his mechanic to your field.

Once the phone rings and interest is shown the game changes. This is not about being nice and making new friends, although we need as many friends as we can find, this is all about selling an airplane, your airplane.

ABC!

Which stands for, <u>A</u>lways <u>B</u>e <u>C</u>losing.

The first paragraph you speak to an interested party on the telephone has to include this phrase, "Have you got your money together?" or "Is this purchase funded?" if you prefer.

Everything you say after answering the phone must qualify the prospect and call for commitment. **"Is this purchase funded?"** cuts to the chase for you and the prospect.

It says loudly, **"Are you ready to buy or are we just wasting each other's time?"**

It is a very fair question and sooner or later you gotta' know if this guy can perform on his aspiration to buy not simply talk about buying your airplane. He knows whether or not he can afford an airplane and whether or not he's prepared to act. Before spending a lot of time with him you need to know as well. While you're on the phone with a *"Lookie Lou"* a real buyer may be on call waiting.

Move quickly to handling objections by opening the door.

"What most concerns you about my airplane?'

If you are selling a Cessna 150 and he is concerned about it only having two seats, the chance of selling to this man is very, very small. The question, **"What most concerns you about my airplane?"** further sifts the wheat from the chaff. First, it allows you to know who is serious and who is daydreaming. Second, it lets you know if you can positively address his major concern.

If your plane has had some damage history, let's say a gear up landing and he is concerned about that you must establish whether this is a concern that he can move beyond or if he will forever be haunted by it. Is it a negotiating ploy or is it a hard and fast concern? If it is the later you must get it all on the table with a nice open ended question.

"What about that *(the gear up landing)* **concerns you?"**

Let him spill his guts and then answer his objection as best you can and attempt to close with a nice yes or no question **"are you comfortable with what I've told you?"**

If his answer is yes then most people would say, "Great, what's our next step?" You know better as that leaves all of the control in his hands. You're selling the plane so you must take control and never give it up.

"I have always used ABC Aircraft Escrow Company. Is that good with you?"

Notice this is a nice yes or no question. It is designed to close on a minor decision. You cleared up his number one objection and are now ready to sell him the airplane. He has never seen it, or touched it, or flown it or had it inspected. Is he likely to close this easily and this early? No, he isn't but it does sometimes happen.

What you are trying to do is establish commitment and keep the purchase concept on the front burner. You are not two guy's doing some hangar flying; you are a seller and he is a buyer. He can't be anxious to buy if you're not anxious to sell.

Clearly, an interested party is going to ask to see more pictures. The problem is so will a *"Lookie Lou"* how can you know the difference?

Easy.

Before you give him the URL where more pictures can be viewed quickly ask **"I am making appointments for people to see the airplane and have a slot open the day after tomorrow at 2 o'clock in the afternoon. Can you be here?"** If he says no propose another time on another day. If he says no again and doesn't offer an alternative, thank him for calling and say goodbye. If he is a prospect, he'll jump in and affirm his interest by saying something like "I am very interested in your airplane. I would like to see more pictures first if you have them and then I will call you back and arrange a time to kick the tires."

Your next move is obvious, you explain "I understand and I want you to see more pictures of this airplane. I also want you to have a chance to buy it. Others are already making appointments to come and see it. This airplane is likely to go quickly. Look at the pictures tonight and get up here as quickly as you can. I do have the 2:00 PM slot available the day after tomorrow. If you're really interested you should take it." Then give him the URL and say nothing else.

If he's a *"Lookie Lou"* he'll thank you and say good bye. If he's a prospect he'll get down to the business of picking a time.

Chapter XII

Sealing the Deal

The BIG Idea: Match aspirations to specifications by managing expectations.

One of the best merchants in the history of earth was Chicagoan Marshall Field. What made the department store that bore his name so great was one simple phrase, **"Give the Lady What She Wants!"** His vision extended far beyond the trinkets on his shelves and the clothes on his racks. He was talking about the entire shopping experience. It was this attitude that caused him to incorporate what was to become a treasured restaurant into his flagship store on State Street in Chicago.

The idea was simple. Don't let them leave the store for lunch. Once they're in the doors keep them there by creating a welcoming environment which includes great food served in an elegant setting with first class service. The restaurant became so celebrated that people actually came to the store for lunch. On the way in or out they bought something as the restaurant was on the top floor and diners had to ride the escalator through eight floors of things they never knew they needed but soon decided they couldn't live without.

Subtlety works. Listen carefully to your buyers. Learn what they need and more importantly what they want and then get it for them.

Some have said that a good compromise occurs when both parties are equally unhappy. I disagree.

For me, the only deal worth making ends with both parties being very happy with their end of the stick and feeling that have made a new friend. If it looks like you're not going to land at this spot then walk away. Life's too short.

There are two stances that you must never accept to make a deal work.

First you can't be demanding and take a *"my way or the highway"* position.

Nor can you assume the posture of a *"door mat"* and let your prospect walk all over you.

Between these two extremes is the land of compromise and mutual satisfaction.

In the chapter **"What's the Deal?"** we laid out all of the elements of any aircraft sale. To refresh you, here's the list I call it the **Dirty Dozen plus Three**:

1. Who's the Escrow agent?
2. How long from opening of Escrow to closing the sale?
3. Is the sale *"as is"?*
4. Will a pre-purchase inspection occur?
5. Where and by whom?
6. Who pays for the inspection?
7. Who pays for travel to and from the inspection?
8. If repairs are required, who pays?
9. Is the sale *"where is"?*
10. Who delivers the airplane?
11. Who pays the delivery expenses?
12. What is the purchase price?
13. What are the payment terms?
14. Who pays sales tax?
15. Will your attorney formalize our agreement?

Each item of this list presents an opportunity to blow the sale. The best way to proceed is to present the issues one at a time in the order suggested above? Simply ask a question or make a statement that presumes a question and then **"shut up"**.

Listening is the primary skill to be used during negotiations.

Let's unpack the first question, *"Who's the Escrow Agent?"*

The question at once tells the purchaser that you want to use an Escrow company to manage the transaction and that you are willing to consider his recommendation. Chances are very good that he won't have one in mind. This gives you the opportunity to suggest one that you have pre-selected and have already spoken with. Hopefully, you have a good relationship with one and have used them in the past.

The escrow agent will direct both buyer and seller as to what they need to produce, how and when. For a cash deal, he will accept a cashier's check from the purchaser and the executed bill of sale and title transfer forms from you. Everything will be held until both parties tell him that the transaction is complete. He then wires the purchaser's funds to your bank account and files the bill of sale and title transfer documents with the FAA and sends copies to the purchaser. The escrow agent is the expert on how to do the transaction. His instructions should be followed very closely. The process is more complicated if the sale requires the buyer to make payments and the title won't be transferred until he sends the last one. In these circumstances your lawyer is the key.

The escrow agent's first step is to run a title search. That is why the previous chapter titled **"What's the Deal"** advises doing a title search before listing your airplane. Surprises slow things down and make your counter party worry. Don't let that happen. Be researched and be ready!

How long from opening Escrow to Closing the sale?

The second question ties in to the first and sets a tone of urgency to the sale. Listen carefully to what the buyer says. How quickly does he want your plane in his hangar and how quickly can he provide the cash to buy it?

You want a quick close and so should your purchaser. You definitely don't want this to drag on and on. Seven days is more than enough time to open escrow and complete the transaction **IF** things are done in parallel rather than serial fashion. The safety of a third party holding the funds and the Bill of Sale allows the purchaser to deposit his funds before he completes the Pre-Purchase Inspection. The day he decides to pay your price and buy your plane, the escrow account should be opened. It should also be stipulated that if the sale isn't completed with the specified time frame either party may back away from the deal. Urgency gets things done.

Is the sale *"as is"*?

You have done a lot of work as outlined in the "**What's the Deal**" chapter, to prove to the purchaser that your airplane is in excellent shape. Part of that included an Annual Inspection which is now less than one week old. Your purpose in getting everything done is to give any purchaser the realistically **SAFE** option of buying this plane *"as is"*. Additionally you have value priced it at 20% below the market so that the buyer has plenty of room to make any repairs that might later be necessary.

All of the essential steps to prove the condition and worth of the aircraft have already occurred. You have done that so any prospective purchaser can buy *"as is"* with confidence and save valuable time and money in the process.

All that being true it is a rare buyer that will pass up a pre-purchase inspection. His position will be that he appreciates what you have done and accepts that yours is a wonderful airplane and the asking price makes it a great value. Even so he will say that he would feel more comfortable if his mechanic inspects the plane prior to the purchase.

Your retort must be an understanding *"of course, I understand completely. However, all of the expense involved with the pre-*

purchase inspection must be borne by you as I have already spent a greater amount of money validating my airplane's condition and done so very recently."

That sets the theme for the negotiations around questions 4 through 7. Everything will be at the purchaser's expense. If he presses on any or all of them you simply reiterate that you have already paid to have the plane inspected and will not do so again. This stance also sets up for the price negotiations that will surely follow.

"If repairs are required who pays?"

His IA will doubtless find something amiss. He and your IA will debate the issue. Let's assume that he does find something that could require attention; your purchaser will expect you to pay for the repair. While that seems logical you shouldn't do it. Instead you should prepare for that outcome before it occurs. When it is decided that a pre-purchase inspection will be performed and that the buyers IA will be doing it, you simply say these words before being asked, **"That works for me, but I want you to know that if he finds anything that affects the airworthiness of my aircraft I will have it repaired at my expense. Anything else is on you."**

That sets a clear boundary. You are guaranteeing an airworthy aircraft not a flawless aircraft. Your tires and brakes are an example. Your IA passed them because they are within tolerance. His IA may well say, "The brake linings are getting thin and should be replaced. The same is true of the tires." But your statement covers this issue. They are still serviceable and do not affect airworthiness hence if the buyer wants them replaced, he must bear the cost."

Is this sale *"where is"*?

Yes and you must handle the matter delicately. The purchaser is surely going to want to have the plane flown to his airport for the pre-purchase inspection. You explain that you are actively trying to sell this airplane. Other potential buyers are coming to inspect the airplane and make backup offers should his deal fall through. You don't expect that to happen but your only interest is in selling the airplane. Secondly, you want to put as few additional hours on it as possible and you do not want to introduce a maintenance issue that doesn't currently exist. Every flight places wear on every part and airplane parts can break at any time.

You invite the purchaser to schedule a time for his IA to make the inspection at your airport and ask how much time he feels will be needed. If he happens to live close by and points out that his airport is only fifty miles away, you must respond that is a good thing as his IA won't have to travel far and will be away from his shop for a very short period of time.

Who delivers the airplane?

Who pays the delivery expenses?

These two questions are best handled together. You offer quickly to deliver the airplane anyplace in the United States for expenses. Just to seal the deal you comment,

"I love flying this airplane every chance I get. Getting to do it on somebody else's nickel is a chance I can't pass up."

What if he wants to come pick it up and have you pay for his expenses?

Simple!

You decline the offer and reiterate that selling him the plane at the price offered is the only financial accommodation you are able to make. Remind him, that your airplane is being offered at 20% under the average asking price for similar airplanes.

What is the purchase price?

Handle everything else, if you can, before coming to rest on this point. The key to successful negotiations is to get the prospect to take mental possession before you debate the cost of ownership. Prospective buyers will pose this question in many different ways but in the end it always comes out sounding something like this, **"what is the least amount of money you are willing to accept for this airplane?"**

Without appearing to be offended in anyway at all you answer the question with a question, **"Considering that the average asking price for an airplane like mine is $22,000 and knowing that my airplane is extra-ordinary in every way, why do you not think it is worth every penny of the $17,500 I am asking?"**

Listen to his comeback but stick to your guns by saying, **"I do not like to haggle so I priced my airplane at the lowest price I am willing to accept to part with it. My lowest price is $17,500."**

Who pays sales tax?

"Sales taxes are always paid by the buyer on everything. Airplanes are no different."

Will your attorney formalize our agreement?

The final question is merely an offer and a statement. You are telling the buyer that you would like to reduce everything you have agreed on to writing and that you would like to use a qualified attorney to prepare the agreement. You will cover the cost if it's your attorney. He can cover it if it's his. Hopefully both of you will walk away with equal legal bills as either party will have the agreement prepared by the other's attorney cleared by his own. Offering to pay if you get to choose is a good way to go.

Appendix A

Aeronca Aviators Club	www.aeronca.org
National Aeronca Association	www.aeroncapilots.com
America Bonanza Society	www.bonanza.org
American Yankee Association	www.aya.org
BeechTalk	www.beechtalk.com
Cessna 150/152 Club	www.cessna150152.com
Cessna Owners Organization	www.cessnaowner.org
Cessna Pilots Association	www.cessna.org
Cirrus Owners & Pilots Assoc.	www.cirruspilots.org
Citation Jet Pilots	www.citationjetpilots.com
Ercoupe Owners Club	www.ercoupe.org
International Comanche Society	www.comancheflyer.com
Malibu/Mirage Owners & Pilots	www.mmopa.com
Taylorcraft Foundation	www.taylorcraft.org
Twin Cessna Flyers	www.twincessna.org

Appendix B

Sport Aviation	www.eaa.org/sportaviationmag
Plane & Pilot	www.planeandpilotmag.com
Aviation Week	www.aviationweek.com
AvWeb	www.avweb.com
Light Sport & Ultralight	www.ultralightflying.com
AOPA Pilot	www.ultralightflying.com
Flying	www.flyingmag.com
General Aviation News	www.generalaviationnews.com
Kitplanes	www.kitplanes.com
By Dan Johnson	www.bydanjohnson.com

Appendix C

The Controller   www.controller.com

Trade-A-Plane   www.trade-a-plane.com

Aircraft Shopper Online   www.aso.com

Aero Trader   www.aerotrader.com

Barnstormer   www.barnstormers.com

Global Air   www.globalair.com

AeroTrader   www.aerotrader.com